HOW TO STAY UNION FREE

GORDON E. JACKSON

Management Press, Inc.

How To Stay Union Free

Published by Management Press, Inc.

Library of Congress
Catalog Card Number: 78-61773

ABOUT THE AUTHOR

GORDON E. JACKSON is a labor relations attorney who specializes in combating union organizational campaigns and developing programs of union prevention. In addition to his book, *HOW TO STAY UNION FREE,* he has co-authored *WHAT EVERY UNION FREE SUPERVISOR SHOULD KNOW ABOUT UNIONS* and designed *A UNION VULNERABILITY AUDIT FOR THE UNION FREE EMPLOYER.*

Mr. Jackson is a frequent speaker and lecturer on the **Union Free** philosophy at Labor Relations Seminars and Conferences. He handles labor matters and union prevention programs for a variety of industries, businesses, health care facilities and other institutions from a base in Memphis, Tennessee, where he is a partner in the law firm of Jackson, Yeiser and Forman.

Mr. Jackson is a member of the Labor Law Section of the American Bar Association, and a member of the American Society of Hospital Attorneys of the American Hospital Association.

ACKNOWLEDGEMENTS

To all the friends and clients who have encouraged me to codify the **Union Free** philosophy into this book.

To all the many businesses and institutions which I have counseled through the years who have shared and implemented the **Union Free** concept.

To my law partner, Ted M. Yeiser, Jr., whose moral support and superb writing skills helped meet the publisher's deadline.

To my law partner, Michael R. Forman, whose administrative coordination made the book possible.

To my secretarial staff, Beverly Patterson, Jo Thrasher, Kathy Taylor and Evelyn Gaines, who worked tirelessly in their efforts toward *that* final revision.

To Ms. Joan Beifuss whose editing skills were so helpful.

To Juli, Eric and Amanda for playing quietly — sometimes.

CONTENTS

FOREWORD

Statistical sources reflect that a unionized employer will pay an average of 25% more in labor costs than a **Union Free** employer. This average 25% increase in labor costs does not take into consideration any increase in wages or fringe benefits. It is merely representative of the additional costs necessitated by "fooling" with a union. It reflects the costs associated with negotiations, grievances and arbitrations, strikes, sabotages, loss of sales, services and customers, and the inefficiencies and "featherbedding" that creep into a unionized operation.

Assuming your annual labor costs as a **Union Free** employer approximate $400,000, unionization of your facility could easily cost you an additional $100,000—perhaps most if not all your annual profit. Assuming you are a larger **Union Free** employer with labor costs of $2,000,000, union encroachment could raise your costs an additional $500,000.

The less fortunate employer who cannot sustain such increased costs become another statistic—in the bankruptcy courts.

Sometimes more delibitating than the monetary costs to an employer is the sudden realization that it has taken on an unwanted partner when its **Union Free** facility is suddenly unionized.

This is the unwanted partner who attempts to establish or change policies (a responsibility previously held sacrosanct by the employer) without suffering any of the consequences; who, without sacrificing any union revenue, attempts to determine whether and to what extent an employer is going to stay in business; who takes all the credit for employee wage and fringe benefit increases without contributing one cent toward the employees' welfare; and who, without sharing any of the expenses, frequently becomes the depository of contributions made by the employer for its employees' health and pension programs.

Equally damaging to employers who are unionized is the dichotomous "we-they" syndrome devised by union strategists. It is necessary for a union to create a division between management and the rank and file employees in order for the union to justify union dues and assessments from employees. The union must continue to condition its members to the precept that without the so-called "protection" the employee would be forever persecuted by the employer.

Therefore, the traditional "esprit de corps", teamwork and camaraderie enjoyed by the **Union Free** employer between its management team and rank and file employees frequently deteriorate into subtle, psychological warfare once the union forces invade the employer's premises.

Probably nothing frightens an employer more than a strike or work stoppage brought about by unreasonable union demands. Should the employer resist, it may well be faced with a strike and the possible consequences of lost sales and customers, property damage, threats, harassment, personal injury, and closure of the struck facility. Should the employer "cave-in" to unrealistic and irresponsible demands by the union, it may well find that its lack of profit ultimately results in the closure or liquidation of its business, the fear of which may have motivated capitulation to the union in the first place.

Thus, unionized employers pay approximately 25% more in costs; work with a most undesirable, unwanted partner; have to attempt to overcome the union-imposed schism between the management team and rank and file employees; and are placed in the unenviable position of either giving in to unreasonable union demands or, alternatively, facing the consequences of a union strike. The **Union Free** employer simply does not face these problems.

It is a small wonder then that non-union employers desire to remain **Union Free**. The more perplexing question is "How"?

This book will set forth a system which will enable employers to remain **Union Free**. The system is comprised of Ten Master Keys — ten separate steps toward achieving "non-union" status on a permanent basis.

But, **Union Free** is more than "non-union". **Union Free** connotes a positive concept. **Union Free** emancipates the employer, the supervisors, and the employees from the dangers and disadvantages of union-caused problems.

Remaining **Union Free** is both a science and an art. The science encompasses the policies, procedures and programs necessary to afford a firm, fair and equitable system for all; the art concerns the creative use of a multitude of human relations skills in the implementation and administration of **Union Free** principles.

It is most important to note that the causes of unionization and the principles used in avoiding them are applicable to the entire spectrum of employers. Whether the organization is an industrial plant, a health care facility, a financial institution, a warehousing operation, a retail market, a municipal corporation, a state government, or any other type of employer, the Ten Master Keys to maintaining non-union status apply equally to all.

Chapter 1

Commitment

Unions do not unionize employers — employers unionize themselves.

Many members of management these days are quick to point to and bemoan the multitude of ways in which the control of their enterprise is often usurped by outside parties, particularly federal government regulatory agencies. However true such complaints may be, it must honestly be stated that operating **Union Free** is still a prerogative management retains. Today, an employer can still write its own destiny as to whether it will operate union or **Union Free.**

The cement that goes into building a **Union Free** operation, the strength that flows through **Union Free** concepts derives from one common denominator — genuine and uncompromising commitment to the objective of **Union Free** status.

Thus, the initial step to remaining **Union Free** *is management's commitment to that objective.*

One would presuppose that such commitment exists in the majority of facilities that are non-union in this country, but much of this so-called commitment on the part of management is merely a facade.

Management must be truly committed to staying **Union Free** and willing to pay the "price" in terms of money and time. This commitment must exist at all levels of management from the top to the lowest level supervisor. This commitment and the reasons behind it should be spelled out in policy form and communicated to all levels of management and to employees as well.

Top management must decide that operating **Union Free** is a goal equal to other paramount objectives such as sales, customer service, patient care or production quotas. Without such commitment, management will not devote the necessary day in/day out attention to the effort of staying **Union Free.**

Football coach Vince Lombardi once stated that, "Winning is not a some-time thing, it is an all-the-time thing."

Remaining **Union Free** is likewise a day-to-day, year in/year out, full-time endeavor. It is equally an "all-the-time" thing.

SITUATIONS WHICH PROMPT UNIONS TO ORGANIZE

In fashioning a **Union Free** policy and committing personnel, resources, time and effort to that end, **Union Free** employers should be ever mindful that the union is its natural enemy and that its fortress is subject to an attack at any time. In this sense, unions are like water and electricity; they follow the path of least resistance.

In order to gauge their vulnerability and the degree of commitment and effort that must be directed to the task at hand, **Union Free** employers should be aware of several situations which generally prompt unions to engage in organizational efforts.

(1) *Most obviously, unions will respond to employees who seek them out and ask their help in organizational efforts.* If a majority of employees solicit such aid, then all the better for the union. However, even a small minority actively seeking unionization provides a union organizer with an irresistible opportunity for he has acquired a ready-made base upon which he can work to build the majority support the union needs. The smart organizer knows that for every employee who has reached the point where he is ready to speak out, there are ten more who have reached the point where they are ready to listen.

(2) *Unions attack employers whom they believe will not put up a fight.* An employer that has never implemented a policy of maintaining **Union Free** status is surely "union bait."

(3) *Unions seek out employers that have a reputation of poor supervision, substandard wages, inequitable policies and a host of other negative qualities that will be fully discussed in later chapters.* When an employer has a poor reputation in the community, in the eyes of its employees, and with its local competitors, unions will have no trouble whatsoever in "sniffing out" their next victim.

(4) *Unions seek out employers who have a substantial percentage of employees who will be attracted to union propaganda.* Perhaps such employees are former union members who have been "planted" in the employer's facility for the very purpose of getting the union "in". On the other hand, the employees may merely belong to one of the "types" discussed in Chapter 3, "types" of employees whom the union will be able to exploit into joining its forces.

(5) *Unions attempt to unionize employers in pro-union labor climates more so than in areas in which there are cultural and social pressures working against unionization.* Metropolitan areas traditionally have more unions per capita than do smaller or rural communities. Also, unions generally find it easier to unionize employees in the North and East, as contrasted to the South and Southwest.

(6) *Unions prefer to unionize larger employers rather than smaller employers because of the potential for more members and the resultant larger "take" in dues.* (Unions, however, are becoming more attracted to the smaller facilities because they find them more vulnerable and easier to defeat.)

(7) *Many unions attack employers out of revenge for moving to a new location after a complete or partial closure of a unionized facility.* These so-called "run-away" shops are some of the most vulnerable employers because of the resentment harbored against them.

(8) *Unions find it easier to unionize some types of businesses, in contrast to others.* For example, the railroad industry has been highly unionized for decades; so have many construction crafts. On the other hand, unions have found it most difficult to infiltrate financial institutions and only recently have they made inroads into the health care field.

(9) *Unions tend to refrain from "attacking" employers that are strongly and genuinely committed to a* **Union Free** *environment, those that have backed up that commitment with positive and affirmative steps to assure fair and firm discipline, accessible and responsive supervision, full and open communications, competitive and equitable wages and fringe benefits, and those that honor seniority right and the sanctity of a fair and equitable grievance procedure.*

Certainly, many other factors contribute to a union's decision to attempt to victimize one employer instead of another, but, in the main, the factors discussed above prevail. However, no employer is immune. The amount of vulnerability is merely one of degree. The more vulnerable an employer is when exposed to a union attempt, obviously the more it will need a stronger commitment.

It will be remembered that the first situation listed above which obviously prompts unions to launch organizational efforts was the situation wherein employees actively seek out the union. Certainly, it is important for employers to analyze themselves in light of all the possible factors which might motivate a union to single them out for attack.

Nevertheless, it is especially important for the **Union Free** employer to be particularly mindful of the reasons why its own employees through active solicitation would provide a union with the most obvious motive. In sum, the **Union Free** employer must recognize the reasons why employees actively seek organizational activity or are at least disposed to be easy prey for organizational propaganda.

The basic principle which must be kept in mind is that as a general rule employees who seek out a union do not do so for positive reasons. That is to say, employees most commonly do not seek out a union and eventually vote for a union out of a yearning to be unionized. Rather they seek out a union in resentment of their employer and in response to its failings.

Thus, a union, for most employees who seek one out, is nothing more than a means through which resentment and hostility can be ventilated. The union is not something they crave; rather, it is something to which they resort.

Listed below are "Fifteen Reasons Why Employees Resort to Unionization."

FIFTEEN REASONS WHY EMPLOYEES RESORT TO UNIONIZATION

(1) *BAD SUPERVISION.* Supervision can be "bad" for various reasons, including a lack of any sophisticated or formal instruction in proper personnel techniques and the handling of people.

Mainly, however, "bad supervision" relates directly to unfair and harsh treatment of employees.

(2) *LACK OF FAIR AND FIRM DISCIPLINE.* Not only do employees expect fair and firm discipline, they *demand* it. All human beings wish to live and work within a framework of fair and equitable rules of conduct. Firm and equitable administration in enforcing these specified rules of conduct is equally important.

(3) *FAILURE TO EXERCISE COMPETENT LEADERSHIP.* In the same way that employees desire fair and firm discipline, they also desire their management team to exert and exude competence in management practices.

(4) *LACK OF PERSONAL RECOGNITION.* The emotional need for personal recognition is one of the strongest needs in human behavior. Employees who do not receive adequate recognition are sure to question the feeling of management toward them, and all too often they will turn to unions to force recognition from their employer.

(5) *LACK OF JOB SECURITY.* There are many reasons why employees become insecure in their jobs. An employer may have seasonal work or scheduling problems which necessitate layoffs. In other situations, employees might feel insecure because some fellow employee was discharged for reasons that do not seem just. Anyone who is at all familiar with union campaign propaganda knows that the issue of "job security" is the focus of many union promises.

(6) *LACK OF "OPEN DOOR" POLICY.* When employees are treated harshly and unfairly by their immediate supervisor (see (1) above), unless they have a means of "getting around" the supervisor to talk to higher management, these employees may feel that they have no choice but to vent their frustration through some outside third party, namely, a union. Therefore, not only must **Union Free** employers have an "open door" policy — they must keep the door open.

(7) *FAILURE TO HELP EMPLOYEES IDENTIFY WITH THE EMPLOYER.* Employees who do not feel a part of the overall mission and objectives of the employer and are not allowed to "participate" in the fulfillment of the employer's mission and objectives cannot reasonably identify with the employer. The departure from the "family" concept in management frequently results in a feeling

that there are two opposing forces — management and labor. The all-too-frequent consequence is a turn to the union by the employees to satisfy their need to "belong".

(8) *FAVORITISM.* Many union drives have been initiated strictly because of supervisors "playing favorites" among the rank and file. To be less than consistent in the treatment of each and every employee in each and every situation is always an open invitation to third party representation.

(9) *LACK OF (OR INADEQUATE) EMPLOYEE BENEFITS.* Most employees do not seek out a union because of benefits if their benefits are in the "ball park" and comparable to those of other employers in the area. However, when there is a substantial disparity in benefits compared to those of other employers, employees do seek out unionization in an effort to "close the gap."

(10) *SUBSTANDARD WAGES.* To the same extent that employees seek out unions because of inadequate benefits, they seek out unions when their wages are substandard.

(11) *FAILURE TO PUT PERSONNEL POLICIES AND EMPLOYEE BENEFITS IN WRITING.* Not only will employees seek out a third party representative because of the lack of personnel policies and employee benefits, but employees often contact unions in an effort to force the employer to put policies and benefits in writing.

(12) *LACK OF RECOGNITION FOR LENGTH OF SERVICE.* Major organizations in this country have long had specific programs to recognize and commemorate an employee's length of service. Seniority rights, additional vacations, pension programs and the like all go to show proper respect and recognition. Longevity pins and awards are also beneficial methods by which to fulfill this obligation.

(13) *CURSING EMPLOYEES.* Many managerial and supervisory personnel too frequently use "earthy" language in and around their fellow workers. Perhaps most of the "cursing" is directed at the situation, but many rank and file employees feel that the language is directed at them. Also, there are too many situations when the supervisor actually does "curse" the rank and file employee. In such event, the employee might feel that a union would serve to protect him from such treatment by the supervisor.

(14) *FAILURE TO "SELL" EMPLOYEES ON THE BENEFITS AND ADVANTAGES OF WORKING FOR THE PARTICULAR EMPLOYER.* Many employees turn to a union because they have not been "sold" on the various benefits and advantages of their jobs. Not only must employers promulgate their policies and benefits, but they must also "sell" their policies and benefits to the employees.

(15) *FAILURE TO RELIEVE FRUSTRATION AND BOREDOM ON THE JOB.* Managerial and supervisory forces should always be mindful of which jobs tend to be menial, repetitive and boring, and rotate these jobs or, if possible, change job designs to decrease the frustration and boredom elements involved.

These Fifteen Reasons Why Employees Resort to Unionization are certainly not all inclusive. They are merely the most prevalent. Each one will be more fully explored in later chapters. However, they, like the various situations which prompt unions to initiate organizational campaigns, have been capsulized at this early stage in order to give some idea of the scope of the commitment which the **Union Free** employer must adopt.

The commitment must be equal to the task of meeting the challenge of a union organizational effort in those situations which invite such an effort as well as eliminating the various reasons which cause employees to resort to unionization.

It should be quite apparent that the degree of the commitment which is necessary to sustain the "all-the-time" effort to remain **Union Free** must be very high indeed. Further, it should be recognized that each compromise of the effort weakens one's winning edge and increases the vulnerability to union penetration and ultimate defeat.

Therefore, if your organization is unwilling to elevate the goal of staying **Union Free** to the level of its highest priorities, unwilling to abstain from compromises that will deteriorate the commitment and unwilling to devote the necessary time and money to the effort, then read no further. You will be wasting your time.

If you are still reading — "Congratulations". You are on your way to joining the ranks of thousands of management personnel who have decided that staying **Union Free** is worth the effort and who have been most successful in achieving that goal.

The remaining nine chapters will detail the principles and guidelines through which the goal to which you are committed can be achieved.

Chapter 2

The Management Team

"Supervisors either win NLRB elections for you — or they lose them for you."

This statement has been used so many times that for many employees it has become a cliche. However, for the **Union Free** employer it remains something much more. It is a truism worthy of more than lip-service.

Employers who have outstanding supervisory personnel and who have been involved in counter-union campaigns can well appreciate the value of that asset because these employers were most likely winners. Employers who have been through counter-union campaigns and were burdened with unsound, ill-trained and deficient supervisory personnel can likewise appreciate the value of good supervisors, because without them, they most likely lost.

Therefore, the second key to building a **Union Free** *defense is the selection of outstanding management personnel and the training of deficient and unsophisticated supervisors to bring them up to the level required of a* **Union Free** *management team.*

A "fair but firm" management style is the cornerstone of a strong **Union Free** program.

What, then, are the qualities and characteristics of a **Union Free** manager? Of a **Union Free** employee relations manager? Of a **Union Free** supervisor? What factors and points should one consider in the selection and training of management personnel?

The **Union Free** employer must have a selection checklist by which to assure a sound and responsible management team. It must establish safeguards to enhance the quality of front line supervision and it must educate and train its management personnel to their highest potential.

The checklist by which to screen management applicants consists of seven specific tests:

MANAGEMENT SELECTION CHECKLIST

① A new management member should fully understand and appreciate the **Union Free** commitment of his employer and should pledge his individual efforts to that goal.

If his previous experience and training have been in a unionized operation, it should be ascertained that he has the flexibility to operate in a **Union Free** environment and that he is absolutely loyal to the management team. His background should be carefully checked to assure that he will not fall under undue pressure from family members who might be highly sympathetic to the union cause if and when the "chips are down".

② The new member of management should be fully familiar with the various disadvantages of unionization and be able to present these disadvantages to any inquiring employee in order to persuade the employee against union influences.

③ No employee should be promoted into management from the ranks of hourly employees unless such an employee truly qualifies for the position or has the ability to be properly trained for the opening.

More importantly, no one should be promoted from the hourly ranks solely because of his seniority or technical skills. Leadership abilities are much more important to **Union Free** management than technical abilities alone. Obviously, to the extent possible, the candidate should possess both, but if one is to suffer, it should be the technical side. A true leader will be able to make up for any technical deficiency but a purely technical individual will not easily acquire leadership abilities.

④ If the candidate is chosen from the hourly employee ranks, there may well be hostility or jealousy toward him from his fellow employees.

To the extent possible, he should be an individual that his fellow employees unquestionably respect and one whom they would have chosen for the position themselves had they had that prerogative. Leaders surface in the hourly ranks and **Union Free** employers have the obligation of monitoring these informal leaders for possible promotions as well as assuring that their influence over fellow employees is favorable toward their employer and the management team.

5. The candidate must also possess a cooperative attitude and a willingness to be a "team" member. Many talented and otherwise capable new managers defeat their potential contributions to **Union Free** employers simply because they feel an overwhelming need to establish some type of dynasty in their appointed sections. "Empire builders" do not fare well in **Union Free** operations.

6. If the candidate is chosen from outside the establishment and outside the immediate geographical area, assurances should be taken that there are no family complications in moving to the new facility. Obviously, if the new supervisor is burdened at home with expressions of dissatisfaction with the new location, he will have a difficult time in keeping these problems from interfering with the performance of his duties.

7. Whether the selection for the new management member is from the hourly employee ranks or from outside the organization, the candidate must also have the requisite ability to: a) motivate employees; b) sell employees on the organizations's favorable qualities and positive benefits; c) recognize employee unrest; d) be accessible and responsive to employees' concerns, grievances, frustrations and complaints; e) eliminate sources of employee dissatisfaction; f) take an interest in the employees' needs and personal problems; g) reflect an engaging personality; h) instruct clearly; i) make sure the employee understands his work duties and responsibilities; j) constructively counsel and discipline employees for improper work or violations of the rules of conduct; k) sincerely (and lavishly) praise and compliment employees for their good efforts; and l) gain the love and respect of the employees under his supervision.

This management selection checklist should apply equally to each member of the management team.

First, the chief administrator at the facility should exemplify these qualities. He must be accessible for the ventilation of employee concerns, gripes and grievances and he must be responsive so that employee unrest and dissatisfaction is corrected or sufficient explanation is given to satisfy the questions being raised. Succinctly stated, he must be a "people person" first, a "production person" second.

Although it is only good business to be concerned about a lack of efficiency and production and possibly the "over-coddling" of employees, if employees genuinely feel that the management team has their livelihood and welfare in mind, and if they are secure and comfortable in their respective roles, the efficacy of their response to duties and responsibilities will rise to the highest level and they will out-produce any unionized operation.

Aside from the **Union Free** chief executive officer, the second most important individual in a **Union Free** environment is the manager assigned employee relations duties. He may well have the title of personnel director, industrial relations manager, personnel manager, employee relations director or a myriad other titles, but his function, not his title, is the important element in question.

Although some small facilities cannot afford the services of a full-time employee relations specialist, most larger operations provide for such a position. When the facility cannot fiscally justify such a position, then someone in management should be given the responsibility and authority to carry out his functions.

As for the qualities of the employee relations manager, it is much more important to select an individual who is truly personable and engaging and one with a "watchdog" disposition to insure employees' rights and fair treatment than an individual who is merely a "policy writing" expert or someone who is a walking glossary of labor relations laws and requirements.

The better employee relations manager in **Union Free** operations is one who is an "alter-ego" of what a union representative holds himself out to be (but is not). He is truly a spokesman for employee rights and he should have the responsibility of assuring that employees have every penny due them and every benefit available to them. His efforts should be so favorably received by employees that they would not dare substitute for his "good offices" some union representative who could possibly burden them with considerable costs or subject them to strikes and other union-caused hardships.

In a nutshell, the **Union Free** employee relations manager should be a human relations master.

The most important individual on the management team having a direct relationship with the employee is the front line supervisor. As mentioned, in NLRB elections in which employees vote to determine whether they desire a particular union, the front line supervisor is a "maker or breaker." Certain types of supervisors possess characteristics that are most counter-productive to **Union Free** objectives.

In this connection, the author has observed seven types of managers and supervisors who either outright trigger a union campaign that grows out of resentment from employees under their direction, or who are more indirectly responsible for union victories. As an added safeguard to the management selection criteria, these types of managers and supervisors should be either screened out from the **Union Free** employer or, alternatively, be closely monitored and retrained so that their habits can be expeditiously corrected.

SEVEN TYPES OF SUPERVISORS WHO CAUSE UNIONIZATION

1. **The "Boss" Manager/Supervisor.** This type of supervisor is on an ego trip. His nature is to remind employees constantly that he is the boss. He pushes instead of leads; he "orders" instead of requests an employee to do a certain task; and he stresses "you do" instead of "let's do".

The "Boss" Manager/Supervisor is the traditionally militaristic, arbitrary, capricious manager who is generally despised by the employees under his control and disrespected by his fellow management associates. His pomposity, impulsiveness, and gamesmanship is a "turn off" in **Union Free** management. No matter what his experience, background or expertise might be, a **Union Free** employer cannot afford his services.

2. **The Insecure Manager/Supervisor.** This type of manager/supervisor is one who is unable to identify with the role of management. He doesn't want to make anyone perturbed at him in fear that he will not be liked, and, consequently, is unable to demand proper performance from employees. He is the type of manager who not only has difficulty making a decision — due to a lack of confidence — but is afraid to administer the crystal clear policies that are already in effect.

His lack of identity with the management team results in his "passing the buck" and blaming and criticizing other management team members to his employees. His desire to be ever-popular and his inability to stand up for management policies places him squarely on the "unwanted list" when it comes to **Union Free** defenses.

3. **The Inconsistent Manager/Supervisor.** The Inconsistent Manager/Supervisor probably wins more votes for the union than all the other types here discussed.

Not only is this type of manager inconsistent in his administration of policies and practices, he likewise possess a "Dr. Jekyll/Mr. Hyde" personality in dealing with employees. Consequently, employees do not understand him, do not respect him, and are fearful of his actions. His inconsistency is most vividly reflected in his methods of playing favorites with employees under his control and direction.

Again, a **Union Free** employer cannot afford the luxury of having this type of manager aboard its **Union Free** ship.

4. **The Dishonest Manager/Supervisor.** This type of manager is clearly recognizable as one who would sacrifice employees' good will for his own selfish motives. He is the type of supervisor who intentionally misleads employees into believing that the employee is to gain some advantages by "catering" to the supervisor's whims when such is not the case.

The Dishonest Manager is a gossiper, spreader of half-truths, innuendos and slanderous inferences to booster his own self-purpose and vanity. He is a meddler and a perpetual rumor mill. The Dishonest Supervisor's biggest fault is that he is a promiser — without any intention of fulfilling his promises, or, worse, without possessing the sufficient authority by which to carry out his promise.

A **Union Free** facility can ill-afford the Dishonest Manager/Supervisor.

5. **The Cursing Manager/Supervisor.** This type of manager frequently possess many assertive and enthusiastic traits that are very positive qualities. However, many of these positive traits are overcome by his habitual practice of cursing in the presence of employees.

Although such a supervisor might be directing his "venom" at a machine or some other impersonal object, employees in his presence frequently infer that the profane language is directed at them individually. Whether employees lose respect for a cursing supervisor because they feel the profanity is directed at them personally, or whether they generally do not appreciate the use of such language in their presence, the result is the same — the lost respect for the supervisor. (Cursing was one of the Fifteen Reasons Why Employees Resort to Unionization, as discussed in Chapter 1.)

6. **The "Playboy-Playgirl" Manager/Supervisor.** The Playboy type of manager is one who thinks the suprvisor's position entitles him to additional fringe benefits and special favors from those employees of the opposite sex under his direction. This type of supervisor abuses his duties and responsibilities by taking liberties and advantages of his position. He rapidly loses credibility and respect from the remainder of his employees.

He typically makes two mistakes, both of which are reflections on his employer. One, he believes that no one knows of his extracurricular escapades, which is usually a far cry from reality; and, secondly, he feels that he can separate his job from the emotions resulting from such a relationship, which is again very unlikely.

7. **The Reactionary Manager/Supervisor.** The Reactionary Manager is recognized by his negative attitude. He plays "devil's advocate" to every new idea that has surfaced in the last decade. He opposes improvement; he opposes changes; he opposes suggestions or ideas. His attitude is that "We've always done it this way." His lack of enthusiasm and initiative destroys the morale fiber of the employees under his direction. He typically is a manager who is just hanging around to retire — or to find another job. **Union Free** employers should make sure he gains his wishes by an early retirement or less tactful removal.

To be sure, the writer recognizes that the foregoing list involves a degree of stereotyping. Obviously, many human beings possess to varying degrees all or at least some of the traits referenced above and it would be for a trained behavioral scientist to explain why this is so. Nevertheless, the important point to be made here is that if any of these traits are present to a substantial degree in a supervisor/manager, corrective action is mandatory for maintenance of a **Union Free** environment.

Chapter 3

The Employee Complement

Whether a facility has ten employees, or ten thousand, union avoidance is a "numbers game".

First, for those employers who fall under the National Labor Relations Board (NLRB) jurisdiction, a union must obtain authorization cards from at least 30% of the employees before the NLRB will order an election. Secondly, assuming a union does have at least 30% of the employees "signed up" and the NLRB orders an election to determine whether the employees desire a union, the union must receive a majority of votes from the eligible employees voting before it can become the exclusive collective bargaining representative of the employees at which point an employer would be forced to recognize and bargain with the union.

If a union is unable to convince at least 30% of the employees at a **Union Free** facility into signing union authorization cards, the employer remains **Union Free**. If a union fails to obtain a majority of the employees' votes in an NLRB conducted election, the employer remains **Union Free**. Better yet, if there is never a union attempt, the employer remains **Union Free**.

In a nutshell, it is the employees who will *directly* determine whether or not the employer will remain **Union Free**; it is the disposition of employees toward unions combined with the employer's treatment of employees that will *indirectly* determine whether or not the employer will remain **Union Free**.

The ultimate objective then is to have employees who will refrain from signing that first union card. If this can be accomplished, the war is won without the first shot being fired.

The third Master Key to maintaining **Union Free** *status therefore lies in the selection of employees who will neither feel the need for a union (because of good management and fair treatment) nor be at-*

*tracted to a union at a later date because of their latent behavioral
characteristics and behavioral patterns.*

Union Free employers should be aware that it is a violation of
the National Labor Relations Act to fail to hire an employee because
of his union background or sympathies.

However, the law does not require an employer to hire
employees who are unproductive, troublemakers, injury fakers,
morale destroyers or similar "problem" employees. It does not require employers to hire unreliable or irresponsible employees. It does
not require the employer to hire employees who possess low self-
esteem.

Each employee hired is a potential "rotten apple" that may spoil
the proverbial barrel. A single employee can wreak havoc in a union
campaign.

This is the exact reason why an employee relations manager, as
well as the entire management team, must be truly expert in the selection of proper employees.

The employee relations manager must be educated in every facet
of the employee selection process. He must be "schooled" to interview in depth so as to assure the procurement of the most productive,
positive, and responsible employees available. He must have the
resources and the know-how to fully investigate the work record and
background of every employee seeking a job. He must know how to
ask "open ended" questions of applicants so as to afford an applicant the full opportunity of expressing his true motivations, desires
and abilities. (Examples of "open ended" questions are discussed in
Chapter 5).

Equally important is the patience required in the selection process. Production and operations personnel must understand that it
takes time and effort to screen and to hire responsible, efficient and
positive employees. Managers and supervisors who "cry" for more
bodies instead of carefully selected employees greatly jeopardize and
compromise the **Union Free** commitments.

Most important is the obligation and the responsibility of the
employee relations manager and other management personnel involved in the screening of the rank and file employees to recognize
the types of employees who are most frequently exploited by union
organizers, and who are most frequently attracted to union causes

(even though they possess no union background or sympathies at the time of their application or interview). As with the types of supervisors who cause unionization, the author has observed and identified seven types of employees that are pre-disposed to unionization and are therefore invariably exploited by union organizers.

SEVEN TYPES OF EMPLOYEES THAT UNIONS EXPLOIT

1. THE INEFFICIENT, LOW PRODUCTIVE EMPLOYEE. This type of employee realizes that he will not be able to measure up to the facility's standards and will be terminated because of his lack of qualitative and/or quantitative efficiency.

The union organizer seeks out such an employee and this type of employee is mutually attracted to the union because the union convinces the employee that it will "save" the employee's job and clothe him with the so-called shield of "union protection" and "job security".

2. THE INDEPENDENT, HAPPY-GO-LUCKY EMPLOYEE. This type of employee has no great financial obligations or commitments. He typically lives with his parents or is basically supported by someone else. He has nothing to lose by joining up with the union forces. He can survive through the longest of strikes and responds to the union propaganda of "everything to gain, nothing to lose."

If he, in fact, loses his job in a union-caused strike by being permanently replaced or because the facility closes down, he suffers no real consequences because he did not depend on the job in the first instance.

3. THE REBELLIOUS, ANTI-ESTABLISHMENT EMPLOYEE. This type of employee is attracted to the union cause and is subject to union exploitation simply because he opposes everything associated with the establishment. Since most businesses and structural organizations are associated with the "establishment", he is opposed to all management or bosses.

He consequently becomes an antagonist to the employer and a respondent to the union propaganda. (Ironically, he will later turn against the union also because he will eventually come to resent the authority of the union. Unfortunately, this phenomenon will not occur until after he has exhausted all efforts to unionize his employer.)

4. **THE SOMETHING-FOR-NOTHING EMPLOYEE.** This type of employee is the typical injury-faker who has collected workmen's compensation from most of his former employers. He is the type of individual who is always looking for a deal. He takes every imaginable shortcut available in his job and sincerely feels that the world owes him a living.

He is the type of employee who "fudges" on his sick pay or funeral leave and bends every rule to "squeeze" a little more out of his employer. He will obviously be attracted to the union propaganda that he has "everything to gain and nothing to lose." He will completely be sold on the union's typical promises of more money, more fringe benefits, and more of everything. He will not inquire as to how the union plans to deliver nor will the employer's comments on the disadvantages of unionization touch a responsive chord in him.

5. **THE CHRONICALLY DISSATISFIED EMPLOYEE.** This employee might well be one of the most efficient and productive employees at any establishment. But this employee will find fault about everything associated with his employer. He is a hopeless griper and complainer as distinguished from a constructive critic. He is never convinced that his employer is looking out for his interests or the interests of his fellow employees.

He is truly an unhappy individual. He probably was born unhappy, is going to die unhappy, and is going to be unhappy for the duration between. This type of employee is a morale destroyer. He keeps everybody around him continually upset and agitated. It is a fulltime job to dispel his negative rumors and ill-founded remarks concerning the management team.

This employee will be attracted to the union campaign because the union will listen to his gripes and complaints. The union will convince the employee that it will "straighten out" the employer to his satisfaction. The damage is compounded, however, because this individual will reveal every skeleton in the employer's closet out of which the union will further propagandize its cause.

6. **THE CAUSE-ORIENTED EMPLOYEE.** This employee will "jump" on any bandwagon that passes through his area. He was the same individual who joined all of the "off-beat" organizations in

high school or college. He typically led demonstrations against everything from "red dye" to "ban the bomb"—he once took a trip to India to visit his personal "guru".

One can bet his last **Union Free** dollar that the "cause-oriented" employee will be equally attracted to the union effort if and when the union knocks on the employer's door. He is a frustrated leader. He views himself as a self-appointed "savior" and the union is able to capitalize on his frustrations.

7. **THE OVERLY-QUALIFIED EMPLOYEE.** This type of employee is out of his element. He will attempt to exert influence over his fellow employees in an effort to bolster his deflated ego.

He might well be a Ph.D. operating a grinding machine or a former accountant sweeping the floor, but his station in life has deteriorated to the point that his vanity appreciably suffers.

This type of employee includes the employee who has formerly made substantially more money with previous employers. Both will be attracted to the union simply because the union will offer these individuals the recognition that they seek and will seem to offer hopes of returning them to their previous higher stations in life.

A **Union Free** employer must not be misled into believing that an employee is going to be happy with substantially less money than he formerly made. An employer should not believe that an individual placed in a lower job function than one for which he had prepared himself will be happy.

Certainly, with respect to the foregoing seven types of employees, it is again recognized that a behavioral scientist could have a "field day" expounding on the complex reasons why they are easy prey for a union organizer. Nevertheless, the important point here is that the **Union Free** employer must be ever mindful that the presence of an employee who, as a practical matter, can be categorized into one or more of the foregoing "types" can make the task of remaining **Union Free** much more difficult, if not impossible.

Union Free employers must also be aware of other factors and considerations in building (or rebuilding) a **Union Free** employee complement.

For example, the work force should be balanced with various age groups as well as with employees from different surrounding areas. Attempts should be made to avoid "clustering" of any certain groups of employees.

When the work force is heavily concentrated with any one group of employees, that group has a built-in collective atmosphere and can easily evolve into a "power force". These groups often vote as a "block" in union elections and are frequently difficult to convince that being **Union Free** is a benefit to the employees as well as to the employer.

Union Free employers should consider a policy prohibiting the hiring of close relatives. In some smaller communities the hiring of relatives can easily get out of hand. The disadvantages of hiring close relatives are obvious.

First, if a close relative of one of the employees is rejected as an applicant, although for a good reason, the employer has possibly made an enemy out of the remaining good employee. Secondly, were an employer forced to terminate an employee who had several relatives remaining at the facility, the employer would place himself in the position of making additional enemies. Thirdly, the close relative factor leads to "clustering" and "block voting".

Another factor worthy of consideration is the selection and hiring of older and more mature employees. Older employees normally are more responsible and reliable, and generally blend in well in a **Union Free** facility. (Of course, all employees, no matter what their age groups, should be properly screened and selected for good and sound business reasons).

More mature female employees are normally less influenced by union propaganda than those of a more impressionable age or disposition. Many members or the "fairer sex" do not appreciate the "pseudo macho" overtones of unionization. These types of employees are "turned off" to union violence, strikes, union abuses, and corruption.

Union Free employers should also select employees who will both fear and appreciate the many disadvantages of unionization.

It is most important that the **Union Free** employer be knowledgeable of the various handicaps in belonging to a union. Front line managers and supervisors should be educated as to the many perils an employee faces when a union is injected into the relationship between his employer and himself.

A **Union Free** employer should make an effort to collect and maintain newspaper clippings and other materials showing the many negative aspects of unions. Such materials can be utilized to depict local examples of the disadvantages of unions to the rank and file employees. These materials can also be used in the employer's "subtle but steady" campaigns to depict union dangers.

Obviously employees are not going to be overly interested in the disadvantages of unions to the *employer.* But most intelligent employees will be responsive to legal and factual materials that objectively display union hazards to *them.*

What then are the disadvantages of unionization to the rank and file employees?

DISADVANTAGES OF UNIONIZATION TO EMPLOYEES

1. **COSTS.** Unions are in the collection business. They collect union dues and other types of revenue. Their source of survival is in the revenue they collect from employees, such as; a) initiation fees, b) reinstatement fees, c) dues, d) per capita taxes, e) special assessments, f) strike assessments, g) political contributions and h) fines.

These costs can add up to hundreds of dollars per year for an employee—most of the time paid out for benefits he already had or would have gotten anyway.

2. **INFRINGEMENT UPON INDIVIDUAL JOB FREEDOM.** When an employee works in a unionized facility, the union is the exclusive collective bargaining representative of all the employees in the respective bargaining unit. Employees are thereafter pressured, if not directed, to take their grievances and related problems to the union steward, rather than deal directly with their employer about them. This fact can be most counter-productive and handicaps the employee as well as the employer. Additionally, a union contract may restrict an employee's job duties to the extent that under it, he may have a part-time job as compared to a full-time job previously held when the employer had the flexibility to change employees from job to job to keep everyone busy and get production out more quickly.

3. **DISCRIMINATION AGAINST ITS MEMBERS.** Union members are frequently discriminated against by their union in many

ways. Court cases reveal numerous instances where members have been fined by their union for attempting a decertification petition by which to vote the union out. Members have also received fines, expulsions and terminations as a result of crossing picket lines or failing to pay union dues or attend union meetings. Union members are also mistreated by their unions when they are fined or terminated as a result of their "speaking out" at union meetings. Union politics often result in employee discrimination when an employee loses "favor" with the "group" in power and is consequently forced out of his job so that some union "favorite" may receive it.

4. **ILL-REPUTED ASSOCIATIONS.** The McClellan Senate hearings in the late 50's revealed that a substantial number of unions were linked with the underworld. Recent investigations by the Justice Department's Strike Force on Organized Crime reflect similar associations at the present time.

Whether a particular union is linked to underworld influence or not, most have some element of heavy-handedness which many individuals want no part of. Many employees, when exposed to these facts, recognize that joining a union is a far cry from joining some civic organization or church group to which union organizers like to equate union membership.

5. **UNION RIP-OFFS.** A careful review of most union documents filed with the Secretary of Labor (the LM-2 Form) will reveal that a very small percentage, if any, of the employees' dues money and other contributions will ever be returned to the employee in any form or manner. The money "taken" from employee paychecks goes instead to huge salaries and expenses of union officials and representatives. The money also goes into paying for union conventions, airplanes, automobiles, buildings, and a host of other extravagancies which in no way better the employees' station in life.

Worse, however, is the misuse of union revenue through such corruption as embezzlement, extortion, and outright theft. Some union officials and trustees have so eroded some pension funds that the members' retirement funds are in serious jeopardy.

6. **BOUND BY THE UNION CONSTITUTION.** When an employee becomes a member of the union, he is bound by the union's International Constitution. Such Constitutions typically pro-

vide that local union by-laws must be in conformity with its dictates.

Union Constitutions also typically provide for union conducted trials through which employees can be prosecuted, and if found guilty, subjected to fines, expulsions, and possible termination. Union Constitutions generally place the International Union in charge of disbursing funds such as strike pay and determining the conditions under which a striker may receive strike pay.

In sum, a typical union Constitution is filled with rules which subject the employee, his paycheck and his job to the union's dominion and control.

7. UNFILLED PROMISES. Union organizers "puff" their wares to the extent that they create false hopes in employees. Most organizers are "schooled" in the art of propaganda. They infer the powers of a miracle man.

Impressionable employees to a large extent, and most employees to some extent, are led to believe that they will receive substantially more wages and fringe benefits with a union than they would have otherwise received. These same union organizers fail to inform their prospective members about the "negotiation process" and the fact that employees may lose as well as gain in the negotiation arena. They fail to advise employees that the law does not require or compel the employer to make unrealistic concessions, in fact, any concessions at all. The employer's obligation is only to bargain in good faith.

Consequently, when the employer does not agree to union demands and employees wind up with less than promised—possibly less than they would have otherwise received—the employee has been once again victimized by the union.

8. UNION'S SELFISH MOTIVES. Many unions have been known to swap off employees' wages and fringe benefits for the satisfaction of selfish motives. Such a "sell-out" is frequently referred to as a "sweetheart contract" and may be somewhat beneficial to the employer, but hardly to the employee.

The union is willing to swap off employee wages and benefits for three items in turn.

First, the union wants what is termed a "check-off", a procedure in which the employer will take out union dues and forward them to the union. This saves the union the time and expense of attempting to collect the union dues individually from the employees.

Secondly, most unions are desirous of the employer accepting their respective health insurance and most likely the union's pension program. This arrangement adds additional revenue into the union's purses.

Thirdly, most unions in non-right to work states will insist upon a "union shop" which will require all employees to join the union after thirty days in order to work for the employer. As one might surmise, most unions are willing to give up quite a few employee benefits for a "union shop" article in the contract.

9. STRIKES AND THEIR CONSEQUENCES. Strikes are a great disadvantage to an employee. Once on strike, his paycheck ceases; so do his fringe benefits, if the employer chooses. The employee is not entitled to any unemployment compensation in most states. Many strikers consequently wind up losing their personal savings, their homes, automobiles and more. Entire families suffer.

Frequently, strikers become overly zealous and are subjected to arrests, fines and jail sentences. Strikers are often replaced on their jobs, either temporarily or permanently. Strikers are sometimes forced into crossing a picket line to protect their job from replacements or because of financial distress.

In crossing the picket line they subject themselves to possible harassment, intimidation, threats, personal injury and property damage. They subject their families to the same hazards. If they are members of the union, they also subject themselves to fines when they cross the picket line — fines that have been known to reach into several hundreds of dollars — even thousands of dollars in some instances.

10. LOSS OF JOBS. Contrary to union propaganda, job security does not lie with a union's representation of a certain group of employees — just the opposite. When a union is on the scene, any employee may lose his job in two different ways.

First, in an economic strike, the employer has the legal right to permanently replace a striking employee. The replacement is permanent as long as the replacement desires the job. The net result in many cases is that the striking employee has lost his job to his replacement — permanently.

Secondly, many employers are forced to close their operation as a result of a strike during which they cannot meet customer demands, or because they have been forced into uncompetitive positions due to unreasonable union demands. Whether the employee loses his job as a result of a permanent replacement taking his job or because the facility is closed, the result is the same. The union has indirectly cost him his job.

The **Union Free** employer must not only know what disadvantages of unionization can mean to itself; it has the responsibility of familiarizing itself with the disadvantages and hazards which unionization can mean to its employees. It has the further responsibility of imparting that information to its employees, keeping within legal guidelines, particularly if and when the union knocks on its door.

Chapter 4

Policies, Rules and Regulations

Once an employer has committed itself to **Union Free** objectives and has selected the requisite blend of **Union Free** managers and employees, the foundation and structure of a **Union Free** environment is virtually completed.

But what are the guidelines, rules, policies, regulations and practices through which this teamwork will function? In other words, after the question of "who" is satisfied, the "how" must be resolved.

Thus, the fourth ingredient toward a* Union Free *operation is the implementation of fair and equitable policies, rules and regulations.

Employees, like any other disciplined individuals, appreciate knowing exactly what is expected of them both with respect to their job duties and their personal conduct. Therefore, the employee should be carefully and comprehensively instructed about all facets of his job.

He should be shown how his job duties "tie in" with the entire operation and their importance to the overall function of the enterprise.

His job duties and responsibilities should be codified into a job description of both a detailed and general nature. It should be sufficiently detailed to outline step-by-step each and every function of the job to which the employee is most frequently assigned. However, it should also contain language that the employee's job duties include any and all other types of jobs to which he might be assigned.

Flexibility is one of the many residual benefits of a **Union Free** operation and it should not be jeopardized by limiting employees to one task or one function, a sure method of producing "prima donnas".

The evaluation standards and job performance measurements by which the employee will be "graded" should be fully explained to the employee. These standards should be based upon objective and measurable criteria instead of on such loosely defined subjectives as "attitude," "appearance," "disposition" or "initiative." Such subjective factors can be improperly applied by managers and supervisors and can result in favoritism and other unacceptable practices discussed in Chapter 2.

Management personnel must be educated to administer job performance evaluations honestly and fairly instead of as a tool of individual discretion. Once his job functions and the standards by which he will be evaluated have been explained to the employee, he should be given an opportunity to repeat his understanding of those duties and standards to his supervisor to insure that both are on the same wave length.

The same thorough interchange of communication and understanding must exist in the relationship to the employer's rules of conduct.

Rules of conduct are most important for at least two distinct reasons.

First, without the existence of set rules, it is most difficult to administer a method by which to eliminate "problem employees" and employees who offend sound interpersonal relationships or who inflict damage to the employer's property, reputation or the overall morale of the operation.

The second and related reason that set rules of conduct must exist is that without them it is most difficult to discipline and/or discharge employees in any *consistent* fashion, and consistency is mandatory in order to comply with the various federal and state discrimination laws such as Title VII of the Civil Rights Act (EEO), the Age Discrimination Laws, etc.

What then are the best methods by which to implement rules of conduct for a **Union Free** employer?

The first principle in fashioning rules of conduct is to make sure that they are published and distributed to the employees. They may be posted on bulletin boards, made a part of the employees handbook, or tendered to each employee individually, but proper notice to the employee is essential.

✗ *The second principle in establishing rules of conduct is to make sure a fair and equitable system exists through which the rules of conduct can be consistently administered.* From legal considerations as well as practical applications, it is recommended that the rules of conduct be broken into two sections, one for major offenses and one for less serious offenses.

A breach of a major rule of conduct should subject an employee to automatic dismissal. Examples of major offenses include stealing, being intoxicated on the job, damaging property of the employer, striking a fellow employee. Each employer should set its own standards on what conduct is so offensive as to come under the major offenses category.

The second section of less serious offenses is based upon a progressive disciplinary concept whereby the employee is given a certain number of written warnings before he is discharged. Many **Union Free** employers use a three written warning sequence so that upon the third written warning the employee is subject to discharge. Examples of less serious offenses include tardiness or an unexcused absence, horseplay, over-extending break periods. Again each employer must set its own standards.

It should be recognized that in drafting its lists of major and less serious offenses, an employer cannot hope to foresee and include all types of employee misconduct which may occur. Therefore, in the case of both categories the **Union Free** employer should specifically note that the lists are not all inclusive and that employees engaging in unlisted acts of misconduct are no less subject to discipline. The **Union Free** employer will note those unlisted acts of misconduct which do occur both for the purpose of insuring disciplinary consistency should the misconduct occur again, and for the purpose of including such acts in any redraft of the rules.

✓ Many progressive disciplinary systems for less serious offenses provide that the three warnings do not have to pertain to the same offense to subject the employee to discharge. One warning might be given for taking excessive breaks, another for "goofing off", and even a third for running "bad parts." However, most progressive disciplinary systems provide a method by which written warnings are removed from an employee's file after one year so he can achieve a "clean slate" at some point in time.

Although the author dislikes the utilization of "suspensions" as a method of discipline due to its union overtones and its punitive connotations, it is most important to temporarily suspend an employee during the investigation of the facts in a discharge case whether it is a major offense or the last step of a progressive disciplinary system. Suspension gets the employee off the premises and gives additional and sufficient time in which to fully investigate all the facts to make sure discharge is appropriate.

The third principle involved in the implementation of rules of conduct is to insure the consistent, fair and equitable administration of those rules. This entails the complete understanding of the rationale behind each rule by the entire management team. It also entails proper monitoring and coordination through the employee relations department to make sure that managers and supervisors are not improperly interpreting the rules nor applying them discriminately to suit their own fancies and whims.

Another important element of consistent administration of the rules involves the right of the employee to "grieve" his discipline — which will be fully discussed in Chapter 6.

The fourth principle to be remembered in establishing rules of conduct is that the utilization of discipline in the **Union Free** *environment should be regarded as corrective instead of punitive.* Especially for the loyal and dedicated employee who might have innocently and unintentionally breached a rule of conduct, it is most important that the employee be counseled in the right manner. The less sophisticated manager may well make an enemy out of a very good employee by improper handling of the problem involved whereas a more knowledgeable supervisor may be able to turn the event into a better and closer relationship with the employee. In this connection, managers and supervisors should be cognizant of some basic concepts in correcting, counseling and disciplining employees:

TEN COMMANDMENTS FOR PROPER DISCIPLINE

1. Make sure the employee clearly understood the particular rule in question or the instructions given.
2. The employee should be allowed to explain the reasons for his acts, if any.
3. Avoid using abusive language in the disciplinary action.

4. Discuss the mistake, instead of "running down" the individual.

5. Avoid bringing up past mistakes that have no reference to the situation at hand.

6. Do not discipline and "chew out" an employee in front of his co-workers.

7. Do not call the disciplined employee "names" or refer to him in a ridiculing manner.

8. Do not discuss with other employees the nature of the disciplinary problem of a fellow employee (unless such would constitute a group disciplinary action.)

9. Avoid referring to your position as a supervisor or boasting of your superior position at the time you are disciplining an employee.

10. Some positiveness should be interjected into the disciplinary action as so to reflect the corrective nature of the action as contrasted to the punitive.

The **Union Free** employer must also establish proper rules to limit campaigning on its premises to the fullest extent possible.

First, all persons not employed by the employer should be notified that it is not permissible to solicit employees on the employer's premises. This is best accomplished by placing a sign on the employer's premises to that effect.

Second, the employer must have in existence a legal "no solicitation/no distribution" rule for its employees. It should be noted that the National Labor Relations Act provides employees the right to solicit union membership from fellow employees as well as to distribute union materials to them during break times, lunch periods and before and after work. No rule can prohibit this protected right of the employee. However, the employer can fashion a rule to prohibit an employee from soliciting or distributing union materials during his work time—*and such a rule is a must!* (One should check with his labor relations attorney for proper construction.)

Third, there is no reason why employees should linger around the premises before or after work. Where such practice is condoned during union campaigns, pro-union employees frequently take advantage of this situation and mingle into other shifts to converse with other employees in an attempt to move them toward the union cause. Accordingly, a rule should be implemented that would prohibit employees from being on the premises except during their specific work period, of course, taking into consideration a reasonable time before and after work to coordinate their transportation or other necessary activity.

The policies governing an employee's personal behavior are but a few of the policies and practices that exist in an employee's relationship with his employer.

Policies concerning wages, fringe benefits, promotions, transfers, grievances, seniority, are also important to the employer-employee relationship. And the **Union Free** employer should have two methods of compiling and distributing these written policies and procedures.

First, it should have at its disposal what is frequently referred to as a "policy and procedure manual" for use by management and supervisory personnel. This manual should fully describe all the employer's policies and contain a guideline as to the proper manner of administering them. Each and every policy relating to employee-employer relations should be included in this particular manual.

Second, there should be an employees' handbook for the benefit of the rank and file employees. This handbook should describe the positive benefits that the employer provides to its personnel.

This handbook should also contain a certain amount of "sell" so that the employee can better appreciate the background and history of his employer and the favorable attributes attached to the organization. The only real negative portion of the handbook should be the rules of conduct. But it is most important that the handbook contain such rules so that the employee will be given notice through the handbook of the existence of the rules. In this regard it is advisable that each employee be required to sign for the handbook and told that it is his responsibility to read it.

A "policy and procedure manual" for the management team and an employees' handbook for the rank and file employees reinforce the sound policies already established.

Finally, caution should be taken in changing any policy or in announcing any new policy. Sudden changes in policies affecting employees can cause enormous unrest and insecurity among the rank and file. It only makes good business sense to involve the entire management team in any major decision that might cause employee frustration and it is equally wise to send up "trial balloons" before making a final decision.

Above all, if and when major policy changes are announced, a full explanation should be given employees. Rumors spread and discontent grows when employees feel they are not being given the truth about major changes.

And finally, a cardinal rule of a **Union Free** employer is never to take away an employee benefit once it is given. Once improvements are made in some wage or fringe benefit package, that should be an irreversible decision.

More union drives are triggered by some "unsold" policy change or because employees feel that they have been "cheated out of something" by the employer than any other single reason. *So, beware!*

Chapter 5

Participative Management

Unionized employers function in a hostile and adverse atmosphere. The structural concept of collective bargaining is management versus labor—or vice versa. Often this is more than competitive gamesmanship; it is outright warfare.

On the other hand, a **Union Free** environment is built upon a framework of common purpose. Management and employees share the same objective—survival and growth *for all concerned.*

The **Union Free** environment offers an employee an opportunity to participate in a shared objective. If offers an employee a membership in a team effort. It extends the comforts of working and building together—instead of against.

The chief factor that distinguishes the unionized concepts of antagonism from the **Union Free** philosphy of teamwork is participative management.

Recognizing employees at all levels and allowing them to be a part of the organization is the fifth Master Key to maintaining **Union Free** *status.*

Participative management involves several elements.

The first element is the elimination of the trappings of management as some opposing or superior force to that of the rank and file employees. The divisive and separatist concepts that place management on one side of the table and hourly employees on the other are pure, unadulterated union concepts, rather than **Union Free** philosophy.

Bridging that historical crevice is the first essential in participative management.

Obviously, some prestige and honor should accompany an employee's promotion to the management team. Surely the new position justifies a salary increase and possibly additional fringe benefits as well. But the positioning of management in an ivory tower is counter-productive.

That is not to say that a manager and supervisor should not identify with leadership roles, responsibilities and obligations.

It does mean that a down-to-earth approach and an inclusive "we" instead of "you" should be the requisite management style. It likewise means the removal of such resented trappings as separate lounges and bathroom facilities for the management team. It does mean the removal and elimination of special parking spaces and other rewards given to "special" personnel.

The elimination of managerial trappings includes refraining from constantly referring to supervisors as "Bosses".

Removing the overly-used desk of a supervisor who is supposed to be on the "floor" might be an important move toward participative management. Requiring the employee relations manager to be out among the regular employees could be an additional step toward better employee participation.

The point is simply that a **Union Free** facility cannot afford a division and schism among its management team and its rank and file employees.

After removing the dichotomous trappings that separate the management team from the regular employees, the **Union Free** employer should structure an assortment of communications programs to enhance the desired participative goals.

Sound communication programs serve three vital functions for the **Union Free** employer.

1. Vertical communication programs serve as a monitoring device to detect any supervisory mistreatment or employee unrest. In this connection, the communication program should be so comprehensive and so diverse that no employee would ever feel the necessity of going outside the facility to voice a complaint or ventilate a frustration. The communication program must, therefore, be so designed that the programs will fully ferret out each and every particle of employee discontent.

2. A sound communication program gives employees recognition that they so much desire by making them feel a part of the organization.

3. Communications serve the traditional function of imparting necessary information to employees that will better help them to get the job done.

In a nutshell, communications are the lifeblood of participative management.

The theory of communications is one thing; the function of communications is another. Management communication is primarily the art of listening. Listening is the product of caring and being interested.

Listening is a necessity in accomplishing **Union Free** goals.

Before a manager or supervisor can be in a position to properly listen, he must be accessible to the employees under his direction. He must express to the employees that he is open and is willing to listen to them.

Accessibility is a prerequisite to sound and meaningful communications.

This obligation of accessibility includes the obligation of a supervisor to keep an attentive ear open for complaints and grievances. When the obligation of accessibility is fully acknowledged by the manager or supervisor, the by-product is that thereafter the employee will seek out the supervisor to voice his complaints, frustrations and concerns, instead of "airing" them to some less desired recipient, such as a disloyal fellow employee, his family, the local paper, the community, or worse, a union organizer.

Once the employer has "voiced" his complaint or grievance to the manager, the manager's next responsibility is responsiveness.

The manager is obligated either to correct the problem or explain to the employees why the problem cannot be corrected. In explaining to the employee why a problem cannot be corrected, he should be most fair and convincing in his justifying management's position.

Once the responsibilities of communications are properly understood by the management team, the **Union Free** employer can then design an assortment of communications programs:

COMMUNICATIONS PROGRAMS

1. ORIENTATION PROGRAM. The first communications program to consider is a comprehensive orientation program for new employees. Intense anxiety is normally experienced by any new employee. Great care, attention and patience is required during the early stages of an employee's job.

Many **Union Free** employees have implemented some very sophisticated orientation programs and "red carpet" approaches in an effort to get the new employee off to a good start.

For example, some employers set up a formal "coffee" for their employees and invite the spouses of the new employees as special guests. Top management and key personnel are present to add their welcome.

Other employers have different types of formal in-service orientation whereby the new employee is informed of the employer's policies, rules and regulations. During this orientation procedure the employee is shown the various benefits to which he is entitled. This orientation can be made more interesting by the use of visual aids, graphs, and charts.

Adopting some of the techniques and utilizing some of the communications skills of the marketing team or the public relations department could turn a dull presentation into a very lively one. Salesmanship of the employer's fringe benefit programs should be one of the underlying themes of the orientation process.

Once the new employee is sufficiently and properly advised of the employer's various programs, his supervisor should take the time to introduce him to as many of his co-workers as possible, especially during break periods. Additionally, it is recommended that the employee be assigned a "buddy", normally an older employee, who has the responsibility of also introducing the new employee to his fellow workers and making him feel welcome in his new position.

The "buddy" system allows the employer to associate the new employee with loyal groups within the organization. The properly chosen "buddy" will help sell the new employee on the employer's program and benefits.

Additionally, the supervisor has an enormous responsibility in explaining the employee's job duties to him, explaining the guidelines by which he is to accomplish such duties and making sure that the employee fully understands both.

The supervisor should stress the idea of traditional teamwork shared by both managerial and regular employees. He should reiterate the many fringe benefits to which the new employee will be entitled. Further, the supervisor should inform the new employee of the employer's various communications and employee programs as well as of its open door and grievance procedure.

Moreover, the orientation process should be spread over several weeks for full appreciation and absorption by the new employee. The employee relations manager and the supervisors should be very accessible and attentive to the orientee during this early stage, thus building a better participative relationship.

2. **INDIVIDUAL PERIODIC INTERVIEWS.** The name of the "communications game" is to provide as many programs as possible to allow the employee an opportunity to get everything "off his chest". The periodic interview approach is an excellent method by which to learn of employee problems and correct those problems internally.

Once the orientation process is completed, many managers simply wish the employee a bon voyage and wash their hands of him thereafter. But what about the continuing obligation of the employee relations manager and other key managers to assure each and every employee of their continued care and interest?

Several communication methods will be discussed through which an employer can manifest its interest to its employees. The periodic interview approach is one of the better methods to accomplish this objective.

In the periodic interview the employee relations manager, or some other top administrator of the facility, arranges and invites an employee for a private and confidential talk.

Timetables may vary but one suggestion is that the periodic interview be held on an employee's annual anniversary of employment. It is also recommended that this type of interview be arranged for the probationary employee at the end of his probationary period.

The periodic interview is not a performance evaluation. It is a "chit-chat".

The mechanics of the interview entail bringing the employee into an office and assuring the employee that the meeting is strictly confidential.

The manager's job is to afford the employee an opportunity of voicing any ideas, suggestions or complaints. Suggestions on how to improve the operation of the facility should be welcomed by the interviewer. Constructive criticism is an important element of participative management.

During the periodic interview, the manager should review the employee's personnel folder with the employee and make sure the employee's records are in order. The interviewer should inquire into the employee's attitude toward its fringe benefit package.

The interview should not be rushed or forced. The employee should be given ample time in which to bring to the attention of management any problem that he might have, whatever the nature.

Notes should not be taken at the time of the interview, but mental notes should be stored and written into some form as soon as the interview is completed. These notes should be coordinated with other interviews to determine whether there are any specific patterns of unrest.

For the more socially minded manager or employee relations director, the interview could possibly extend into a coffee break or lunch period.

3. **"ON THE FLOOR" INTERVIEWS.** Interviewers should be educated in the proper methodology of asking questions in order to gain as much feedback as possible from the employee. This art encompasses the ability to ask "open-ended" questions that both fully probe the employee and open into a full discussion of problem areas.

The on-the-floor interview epitomizes the utilization of "open-ended" questions. This same non-leading method of interviewing employees should be used in all interview formats as well, including the initial hiring system.

The employee relations manager normally is the one who conducts the on-the-floor interview although other members of the management team may also participate.

As implied, the on-the-floor interview is conducted at the respective employee's work station by the individual assigned to conduct the interview. In preparation for these types of interviews, the interviewer should prepare a roster of all employees at the facility. He should then divide the employees into blocks of specific number, such as in blocks of ten.

In making up such a roster, many establishments use an alphabetized list of the employees, others the sequence used on time cards. Nonetheless, the roster should be made up so that the "blocks" do not contain a "clustering" of one section or one department.

The ideal concept is for the person conducting the interviews to "sample" as many departments and sections as possible each time he performs this particular mission.

After the roster is compiled and divided into various "blocks", the interviewer should then interview all the employees in the respective "blocks" on some pre-arranged timetable, such as one block per day, until the entire roster is completed.

The on-the-floor interview can serve several functions. It can be used as a method of sending up "trial balloons" to test early employee reaction to some new policy change or policy addition. It can serve to procure suggestions and ideas from employees, and it can be used to seek out negative feedback reflecting some pattern of employee unrest so that employee frustrations can be expeditiously eliminated.

Each employer should devise its own samples of "open-ended" questions that reflect the peculiarity of the nature of its work, its size, and location. "Open-ended" questions must be designed so that they do not elicit a "yes" or "no" type of answer, but force the responding employee to make some type of statement that reveals his feelings concerning the subject matter.

SAMPLES OF "OPEN-ENDED" QUESTIONS

(1) What do you like best about the job to which you are presently assigned?

(2) What do you like least about the job in which you are presently working?

(3) Were you the supervisor of this department or section, what changes would you consider to make the work easier?

(4) What comments have you heard concerning our new insurance benefits?

(5) What can I do as an employee relations manager (or some other position) to make your job more satisfying?

(6) How would you compare your job at this facility with the one you had prior to coming here?

(7) What has most surprised you about your recent transfer or promotion?

(8) What do you feel your fellow employees are most dissatisfied with about this firm?

(9) Were you the owner of this operation, what are the three things you would do to make it a better place to work?

(10) What are the three weakest traits or habits of your supervisor?

(11) What are the three strongest characteristics of your supervisor?

(12) What are your most frequent "pet peeves" in working here?

Each "open-ended" question should be designed to encourage the employee to speak up. Each question should pertain to a subject matter of interest to the employee.

4. COMPLAINT BOX. In addition to the many communications programs through which can be used to elicit direct comments and responses from employees, there should be alternative systems by which to solicit anonymous comments.

Many employees are very uncomfortable in face-to-face interviews and fear possible retaliation for expressing some negative comment about their supervisors or some policy of the employer. Other employees feel that some subject matters are so sensitive that they should not be addressed directly.

The complaint box program is a means of avoiding direct communications but still providing a method through which employees can voice their concerns and complaints.

Because of the various connotations attributed to such terminology as "Suggestions Boxes", the author recommends that some unique title be given to the container in which complaints are placed so that the employees will understand its true purpose. Its purpose is not for suggestions or ideas but for complaints. A less sophisticated term might be "Bitch Box". Or some more creative employer might refer to it as a "Letter of Concern" box.

Regardless of what the container is entitled, there are certain guidelines and principles that must be followed to assure its successful use.

The "complaint box" must be equipped with sufficient paper and pencils so that it will be convenient for the employee to use.

It should be continually advertised among the employees as a means to "voice" complaints and grievances anonymously. A policy should be established so that distasteful or indecent comments would not be considered or responded to by the employer.

An answer to the complaint or inquiry must be furnished the employees and yet the confidentiality of the inquiring employee must be maintained. The employer might respond to the complaint by publishing both the question and the answer in its newsletter or newspaper. Or the answer might be posted on the bulletin board. If the employee has signed his name to his inquiry or complaint, the employer should respond directly to the employee and get his approval prior to publishing the inquiry or posting the answer to it.

If the employees gain an impression that the use of the "complaint box" is an exercise in futility, its effectiveness will be assuredly destroyed. **Union Free** employers should not take that risk but should fully explore the many benefits received from using a complaint box system. This method is one of the few participative methods through which employees can voice their complaints and concerns with anonymity.

5. **THE "HOT LINE SYSTEM".** Some **Union Free** employers have explored additional methods by which to solicit anonymous comments from employees.

One method is to install a telephone service into the personnel director's office or some other monitored location whereby the calling employee can record a message regarding his particular complaint, grievance or frustration. The employee inquiry is then answered similarly to the procedure mentioned above regarding the "complaint box", that is, through the newsletter, bulletin board, etc.

Obviously the cost and administration of this type of system is more involved than a "complaint box". However, its uniqueness and convenience should offset any presupposed prohibitive costs.

One danger accompanying the "hotline" approach is that of its vulnerability to "crank" and "obscene" calls by less self-disciplined employees as well as by non-employees who might obtain access to the particular telephone number.

Otherwise, the approach is attractive and should augment participative communications. After all, if an employee has the availability of "dialing a prayer" or a "suicide prevention center", why shouldn't he have the opportunity to "dial a complaint"?

6. EMPLOYEE ATTITUDE (OPINION) SURVEYS. Another method by which to receive anonymous reactions from employees and a method by which to monitor employee discontent and frustration is the use of what are commonly referred to as Employee Attitude or Opinion Surveys.

This tool of monitoring employee frustration enables the participating employees to "check" a series of answers to questions about such things as supervisor responsiveness, working conditions and safety programs, as well as to give their reaction to the wage and fringe benefit structure at the facility.

Since numerous consulting companies design and conduct such surveys, they come in all sizes, packages and variations.

Employee Attitude Surveys are very beneficial to most employers but are subject to several conditions before their value can be fully realized.

The first condition is the establishment of their use on a continuing and permanent basis instead of the "one-shot" experiment. This is important and necessary so that the facility can compare the degree of employee frustration and unrest in each department and section from year to year or within some other appropriate time frame.

Second, the Attitude Survey should be given on the employer's premises during work time for which the employee should be paid.

The employer, or the individual conducting the survey on the employer's behalf, should fully explain the purpose of the Attitude Survey and the mechanics of the survey to the employees. This instruction should contain the fact that the employees are not to sign their names so that their participation will be confidential and anonymous.

The instructional process should also inform the employee of the beneficial facets of the survey, that through employee participation the employer is attempting to make the facility a better one in which all can work together.

Third, the employer should discuss the results of the survey with the employees and possibly probe further to find the underlying reasons for their responses. This exploration can be focused through "rap sessions", which will be later discussed.

Fourth, the deficiencies brought to light by the employee responses in the Attitude Survey should be suffiently corrected or explained so that the employees will not feel "jilted" by their participation.

The Attitude Survey program is an important communications device and a great tool in augmenting participative management goals. Its usefulness, however, is directly related to satisfying the four conditions mentioned above.

If an employer uses an Employee Attitude Survey merely for the exercise involved, it will be counter-productive as it will only create additional frustration on the part of the employees involved.

7. **SMALL GROUP MEETINGS.** Another tool for meaningful communications between the management team and the employee rank and file is the small group meeting, or what is frequently referred to as a "rap session".

The mechanics of the "rap session" are that the manager of the facility, or perhaps the employee relations director as an alternate, meets with groups of employees numbering in size from five to fifteen for the dual purpose of imparting newsworthy information and seeking out any ideas, suggestions or any concerns or complaints the employees might desire to ventilate through the conversations.

It is important to keep the size of the group small enough so that each person will have an opportunity to participate and will feel comfortable in voicing his ideas and suggestions within the group. A group of more than fifteen employees frequently "dampens" the atmosphere so that the shy or meek employee will not "speak his piece".

For a more effective "rap session" program, the manager or employee relations director who is conducting it should take copious notes during the discussion for later digestion. After rotating the small groups so that all employees of the facility have participated in "rap sessions", the list of suggestions, ideas, concerns and complaints can be compiled into one central analysis.

Thereafter, the management team should use the list of ideas, suggestions and complaints as a checklist for corrective action as well as a guide by which to inform employees of the reasons why certain items cannot be corrected.

An uncompromising law of employee relations is never to inquire into an area of complaint that the employer is either unwilling or unable to do anything about. The employer should explain why it cannot, or will not, take certain actions when employees inquire, but there is no logical or intelligent reason to launch a probe into a sensitive area when management knows beforehand that they can make no changes.

This "cardinal" rule particularly is applicable to "rap sessions".

As mentioned before, "rap sessions" are an excellent forum in which to discuss the results of Employee Attitude Surveys. The small informal setting is conducive for probing further into problems that surface from the survey reports.

Inasmuch as "rap sessions" are frequently used and adopted during a union campaign at employers' facilities, this "small group meeting" concept should be implemented at an early stage, long before the presence of any union attempt.

And, the "rap session" program should be utilized on a continuous basis, instead of haphazardly or intermittently.

8. **STAFF MEETINGS.** Many of the previously discussed programs involve the efforts of the employee relations director or the top manager of the facility, as contrasted to lower management. Such programs are essential since it is so important to eliminate any deficiency in supervision.

However, there are many types of employee unrest and frustration that are not directly related to supervision but grow out of a resentment toward working conditions, policies and other non-supervisory-related elements.

A front-line supervisor has equal responsibility with top management in assuring that the machinery of participative management works. His direct and daily association with his employees is the very force that binds the participative relationship. The supervisors' duties and responsibilities toward eliminating employee discontent and dissension are continuous.

Each supervisor should design his own systems by which to "stroke" or support employees and build a firm foundation of respect and teamwork.

In addition to the methods previously mentioned, many enlightened **Union Free** supervisors implement "staff meetings" for their employees to get the day, or week, off to a good start.

Such staff meetings should have no vestiges or trappings of formality, but should serve to cement the teamwork and family relationship of the group. The "staff meeting" is analogous to the before the game huddle in a sporting event.

The supervisor's "staff meeting" is a forum by which to eliminate employee irritants at an early stage and is participative management at its basic and most important level.

9 EMPLOYEE COMMITTEES. Many **Union Free** employers use employee committees as an additional communications program.

The use of such committees is both dangerous and sensitive. It should be noted that creation of an employee committee that has the recognized power and authority to bargain with the employer or has the influence to adjust grievances with the employer constitutes a violation of Section 8(a)(2) of the National Labor Relations Act on the part of the employer. This arrangement most likely would be considered to constitute a "company dominated union" were the system tested by an unfair labor practice charge.

The first consideration in implementing an employee committee, then, is to assure that the committee has no recognized, or de facto, power by which to bargain or adjust grievances with the employer.

The establishment of employee committees frequently creates jealousies and friction among the employee rank and file. When this occurs, the usual benefits derived from employee committees are destroyed.

Therefore, an employer who desires to use employee committees should build safeguards against potential jealousies and friction as well as satisfy the legal requirements mentioned above.

When these problems are handled, employee committee programs are a great asset in satisfying needs for recognition among certain employees.

Various types of employee committees have been formed through the years, One of the more standard employee committees is a "safety committee" whose purpose is to suggest ideas on how to better improve working conditions and safety features of the operation.

"Recreational committees" are frequently used by **Union Free** employers to allow employees to assist in the formation and "fielding" of employer-sponsored sports teams. Frequently employers create "entertainment committees" so employees can help plan and coordinate such employer-sponsored events as picnics, open houses, and other parties.

Employer newspapers and newsletters need the contributions and input of employees, and, consequently, a "publication committee" is often formed so that employees may assist by submitting news items and coordinating the publication of the employer's newsletter.

The list could go on and on, but the important factor to remember is that employee committees do serve a very beneficial function as an additional communications conduit. When used correctly, such groups can strengthen participative goals.

10. **NEWSLETTERS AND NEWSPAPERS.** An employer's newsletter or newspaper which publicizes what is going on at the local facility and lavishly reports on events surrounding employees is a most useful communication tool to help bring recognition to employees.

Employee participation is an essential ingredient in building a responsive publication. The publication should be oriented to the employees, not to the employer. It should feature as much positive news concerning individual employees as possible, including awards, birthdays, attendance merits, activities. When feasible, it should contain photographs of employees and their families. It should have special interest features concerning accomplishments of employees.

It is an excellent medium through which to communicate a positive image of both the employer and its benefits and to keep the employees fully informed of major announcements. It should contain a column to which employees' complaints, inquiries, or suggestions can be addressed. It should also contain a column under the signature of the top management of the facility written about matters of recent concern.

11. **BULLETIN BOARDS.** Attractive and abundant bulletin boards are another communication tool to which a **Union Free** employer should give considerable attention.

Bulletin boards that are antiquated and unattractive should be discarded and replaced with modern bulletin boards that are specially designed to complement the employer's communication programs. Most modern bulletin boards are displayed in an attractive location, with proper lighting, and enclosed by glass to protect and preserve the contents.

Equally important is the removal of old and outdated material on bulletin boards and a substitution of clean and "fresh" information. The more sophisticated **Union Free** employers go to additional pains in displaying notices that are eye-catching in design and graphics and use the bulletin board to continually inform employees of new policies and events that affect them as well as accentuating the on-going benefit programs.

Some employers set up special bulletin boards on which employees can advertise "sale" items, but caution should be taken with respect to any type of an employees' bulletin board. Employee bulletin boards should be controlled by the employer and monitored by someone from the management team so that controversial materials are not displayed on them.

One of the indirect dangers of an employee bulletin board is that during a union campaign, pro-union employees may attempt to utilize such bulletin boards for displaying union literature and propaganda. Again, if the employee bulletin board is protected by glass and monitored by the employer, union sympathizers will be dissuaded from trying to use the board.

Whether the bulletin board is a regular employer bulletin board, or one for employees, the management personnel in charge of it should have the responsibility of initialing and approving each and every piece of communication placed upon it.

When properly controlled and properly displayed, bulletin boards compliment the communications effort.

12. **MANAGEMENT SPEECHES.** During counter-union campaigns, most labor attorneys and consultants recommend that the employer address the employees in a "captive audience" meeting and make a speech to them concerning the employer's position with regard to the union and the disadvantages of a union at its facility. However, when the top manager of the facility has no past record of making speeches to his employees, the union frequently puts out propaganda that the employer did not appreciate the employees until the union entered the picture.

It is therefore, important that the chief administrator of a facility establish a practice and reputation of speaking to the full employee complement from time to time and utilize the speech-making approach as an additional communication device by which to impart major announcements and important events concerning the operation.

Moreover, the employees appreciate being assembled as a body and hearing from their leader. The very structure of the assembly depicts the team effort and gives added recognition to it.

13. **MANAGEMENT CORRESPONDENCE.** It is equally necessary to occasionally send a letter or some other type or correspondence to the employees' home in an effort to accentuate employee recognition. Again, when the management does not have a reputation of corresponding with employees of the facility, an attempt to do so when there is a union campaign could cause the union to announce that the employer is now sending "love letters", though it never felt the necessity to do so previously.

The more modern **Union Free** employer also takes advantage of the U. S. Postal System in sending remembrances to the employee and his family.

It takes little time and effort, and very little money, for an employer to send a birthday card to the employee at his home. In fact, a manager's secretary can do most of the administration work and it is merely a signature signing process on behalf of the manager.

Congratulations to the employee on his anniversary date with the employer can likewise be communicated through correspondence to the employee's home.

Such communications should be devoid of frivolous intent. They should be sincere and genuine to show the employee that the management does truly care for the employee's association with the employer. Any overtones of artificiality are easily recognized and are counter-productive to the communications efforts.

Correspondence from the top executive of the local facility could also compliment an employee for outstanding performance, perfect attendance, and other achievements.

The advantages in corresponding with employees are three-fold. The fact that the correspondence is sent by someone in high authority lends great credibility to the communication. It is received at the employee's home so that his family can share in his recognition. The employee is able to read and digest the correspondence in a relaxed and comfortable atmosphere.

14. **PAYROLL STUFFERS.** An additional inexpensive method through which to communicate to employees is to place management communiques into the payroll envelope.

Many **Union Free** employers utilize this method to publicize the cost of fringe benefits which are not reflected in the payroll check. Other employers use payroll stuffers to accentrate some type of "in-house" program such as safety, cost reductions, quality control.

The fact that the communication is attached to the payroll check lends additional "clout" to the particular message.

15. **POSTERS.** Posters are an excellent device to dramatize certain campaigns of the employer.

Many posters can be purchased that are professionally drawn and which encourage and emphasize the importance of customer relations, cost reduction, attendance programs, safety programs, suggestion bonuses, and so forth.

Posters should be attractive and informative and placed in locations of easy accessibility. Ingenuity, creativity, and even humor should be used to highlight the themes of the posters.

Finally, it is again important to note that posters are frequently used in counter-union campaigns and the employer should establish an early practice of using them.

16. **EMPLOYEE HANDBOOK.** The employee handbook was discussed in Chapter 4 but it should be mentioned here as one of the most effective communication tools available to inform the employees of various advantages and fringe benefits the employer offers.

The handbook should be designed in an easy to read pattern. It should be colorful, and contain cartoons or some other graphics to illustrate the various subject matters. Employee handbooks are a very important part of the total communications mosiac.

There are several other communications programs through which the participative concepts can be illustrated. But the above-discussed programs are some of the more traditional and more adaptable.

EMPLOYEE PROGRAMS

Another very important element of participative management is that of programs that further recognize the employee and also involves him in friendly interaction with management outside of working hours.

Such employee programs reflect the desire of the management team to share a spirit of brotherhood with the employees. Some of the more popular employee programs include the following:

1. **PICNICS.** There is nothing more refreshing than attending an employer picnic where the employees and their families fully participate in the activities. It is most important that such picnics have the proper planning and that the employer devote sufficient money to promote the picnic to its fullest potential.

The children of the employees should have special entertainment so that they enjoy the function and desire to attend in the future. It is also good for the management team to do much of the physical chores at the actual picnic to show employees that they are working for them as well as with them.

Sporting events and entertainment should be planned to coordinate with the eating time and to assure that the picnic does not "drag" or in some other way become a "bust".

One of the most important elements of a picnic is to have picture-taking of those in attendance. To maximize exposure these photographs should be abundantly displayed in the employee break area, on bulletin boards, and at other accessible sites on the employer's premises. Such photography accentrates the "recognitional" factors.

2. **OPEN HOUSE.** An "open house" is an additional employee program that includes the employee's family. It is one of the few programs through which the employee is able to show his family his particular role in the overall operation of the facility.

The pride that grows from an employee explaining and showing his particular job to his spouse and children is immeasurable and is a lasting catalyst for overall teamwork.

As with the picnic program, the open house should receive the greatest degree of publicity available, with photography and full coverage if possible in the community media as well as in the employer's publications.

3. **BANQUETS AND PARTIES.** Many **Union Free** employers sponsor banquets and parties for employees in commemoration of some outstanding event, or during some holiday season. Such festivities add additional meaning to the participative effort.

The image created by such banquets and "get-togethers" to commemorate years of service, outstanding performances or attendance and retirement recognition contribute toward a team atmosphere, and they are a great boost to employee morale.

4. **SPORTING EVENTS.** Probably no single function creates more of an "esprit de corps" within an organization than the sponsoring and participating in such sporting events as league bowling, softball and similar activities.

While **Union Free** employers are encouraged to sponsor such teams if possible, a word of caution is in order. Such teams need more than sponsorship, they need active support and interest on the part of management.

It must be recognized that the formation of a team obviously generates loyalties and allegiances in and among the team members. Such a group if collectively disaffected with its employer can be a ready made base out of which an organization drive can be built. Certainly, a lack of active employer support could be one source of such disaffection.

Therefore, active support and interest evidenced by employer attendance at and monitoring of team activities is mandatory.

5. **COMPLIMENTARY FOOD.** Employees genuinely appreciate an employer going "above and beyond the call of duty"

from time to time and surprising the employees with such added attractions as "lunch on the boss".

Most communities have catering services or some type of "chicken in a basket" that can be easily brought in to the employees during their lunch or dinner break. The "breaking of bread" among the management team and the rank and file employees adds to the spirit of teamwork and cooperation.

There are many variations of furnishing complimentary food and other related gratuities to the employee at the facility. For example, employers could furnish free donuts and coffee for special events. Candy strategically placed in the lunch or break rooms, for instance, on Valentine's Day is a special favor not easily forgotten, especially by female employees.

These additional "treats" particularly hit a responsive chord when the employees are working overtime or fulfilling some pressurized production commitment.

6. **SERVICE AWARDS.** Longevity and seniority are two very special and honorable attributes of any employee. The pride taken in an employee staying with one employer for any substantial number of years should be recognized and complimented.

A banquet is an ideal method by which to honor employees who have achieved many years with the company or organization. The top executive of the employer should be at the banquet and personally make the presentations and remarks in honor of the occasion.

Loyalty and appreciation is a two-way street. An employee, or a group of employees, who have been shown substantial appreciation by their employer for their efforts through the years most likely will return that appreciation when the "chips are down".

7. **PERSONAL COUNSELING SERVICES.** The **Union Free** employer must understand the "needs" of employees. One of the most prevalent "needs" of employees is assistance in their personal problems. At a minimum, employees desire management to *appreciate* their personal problems. Personal problems might encompass financial difficulty, health or marital problems, or a variety of other emotionally taxing frustrations.

The supervisor who is attentive and responsive to those needs and is able to assist the particular employee toward a proper solution is most likely going to be a lasting ally of that employee. The same is true with respect to an employee relations manager who assists and helps employees in their personal problems.

An employee relations manager, a supervisor, or a top executive who can recite the names of each and every employee in his establishment, the names of the members in the individual employees' families, and any special problems relating to the employee or his family reflects an employer who is going to stay **Union Free.**

For most individuals, their family relationship is the most important factor in their life. When the management team sincerely and genuinely expresses its concern for the welfare of that family and, of course, the welfare of the individual employee, that management team in addition to being rewarded with the great joy and fulfillment that such involvement brings, will also receive the extra bonus of remaining free of union problems.

Personal counseling is the responsibility of line supervisors, middle management, and the top management as well as the employee relations director.

However, personal counseling does not involve the meddling into someone's private or confidential life nor does it entail the gossiping of confidential or controversial matters. But it does involve extending a "helping hand" within the capacities of the respective supervision and management, or the referral to some professional services.

8. **SUGGESTION AWARDS. Union Free** employers should also reinforce their employee programs by offering bonuses or awards for suggestions and ideas toward improvement of the operation.

This type of recognition mirrors the appreciation of the teamwork and effort of the rank and file employee for the overall success of the facility.

9. **COMMUNITY PROGRAMS.** Employers should work with community leaders to the extent possible in an effort to show the employees that they are truly involved in the progress of the community.

This includes ongoing participation in local civic organizations and work with causes for the good of the community. Community involvement also affords a **Union Free** employer an opportunity to continually monitor the pulse of the community and the actions of other employers in the community with regard to union campaigns and union efforts.

Many times, the employer is able to sponsor an employee to work with some community program on behalf of the organization. An employee might be a tour guide for school children who come to the employer's premises for an educational tour. Another employee might speak as a local school on his particular technical expertise concerning a certain product or technique.

Sometimes employees are members or officers of various associations within the community. Often, especially in smaller communities, employees are elected officers of county or municipal government, or are otherwise involved in political activities.

Members of the management team should work closely with employees who exert such leadership qualities. Ideally, these especially influential employees will be particularly appreciative of the employer's programs and policies and will seek to promote them when possible in connection with their outside activities.

10. **EMPLOYEE DISCOUNTS.** Employers have an additional method by which to gain "points" with their employees—allowing them discounts on their products or services.

There are several types of programs regarding employee discounts, but the usual arrangement is that the employee is allowed to buy the product at "cost" or at a certain percentage of the retail price. Some employers make a gift of their product or service to the employee on special occasions such as the employee's birthday or the Christmas season.

Union Free *employers should consider the above programs as only a starter to their own collection of tailor-made employee programs.*

Once the division between the management team and the rank and file employees is bridged, and sound communications programs are established and the employer has implemented a variety of employee programs through which the employees can further participate and gain recognition, there is one remaining element necessary to satisfy the full participative goals of a **Union Free** employer.

The final element is an evaluation system to assure that the communication tools and the employee programs are functioning at the highest level possible.

EVALUATION SYSTEMS TO MONITOR EMPLOYEE PROGRAMS

(a) **EXIT INTERVIEWS.** **Union Free** employers should institute an exit interview program and design an exit interview checklist. Each employee who voluntarily quits his employer should be given an exit interview form to complete for the purpose of determining his reason for leaving the facility.

The employee relations manager, or someone on his behalf, should "probe" deeply into the basic and underlying reasons why the employee is terminating his relationship with the employer. If the interviewer is able to "dig" sufficiently deep, he may well uncover some valuable information which could be utilized in restoring better employee relations.

Exit interviews should be collectively analyzed to determine any patterns or clusters of employee discontent and to discern any breakdown in responsive supervision.

(b) **ATTENDANCE RECORDS.** Attendance records also depict possible employee unrest. A high degree of absenteeism and tardiness is normally indicative of the employees' dissatisfaction with their work, and sometimes their supervisor. Attendance records also should be collectively evaluated so as to monitor the overall effectiveness of the communication and employee programs.

(c) **SAFETY RECORDS.** An increase in on-the-job injuries and accidents, according to safety engineers, mirrors employee unrest to some degree. Theoretically, secure and satisfied employees inject positive responses toward safety programs and are more attentive to the work requirements, resulting in better safety habits.

Although safety records do not reflect as great a monitoring device as exit interviews or attendance records, they do indicate some measure of employee dissatisfaction. Their use should be combined with other monitoring devices for a better measuring method.

(d) **DISCIPLINARY ACTIONS.** The number of disciplinary

and discharge actions are also indicative of employee unrest and frustration. An increase in disciplinary actions may well reflect an internal problem with an individual supervisor or with some unaccepted policy.

The employer should be on the alert for any appreciable increase in disciplinary or discharge actions.

(e) **PERFORMANCE EVALUATIONS.** Assuming that the performance evaluation standards are based upon objective criteria, and assuming further that the supervisors and managers employing the performance evaluation standards are applying them honestly and fairly, a pattern of lower performance evaluations for any group, department, section, or individual, can reflect a morale problem and a deterioration in the communications and employee programs.

Comparative studies of employee performance records from year to year, both individually and collectively, may reveal sufficient evidence that employees are rejecting the management team and its policies.

(f) **ATTITUDE SURVEYS.** Although previously discussed as an excellent communicative tool through which to solicit anonymous reactions and responses the attitude survey is equally a monitoring tool, and when used within the guidelines previously discussed, it is one of the best devices available to evaluate the degree of employee satisfaction with job, money and relationships.

(g) **UNION VULNERABILITY AUDIT.** The exit interview approach, the absenteeism analysis, safety records, disciplinary actions, performance evaluations and attitude surveys, are all tools by which to gauge, to some degree, the effectiveness of the participative management systems. They all have their individual limitations and weaknesses as a means of "checks and balances".

However, the most effective monitoring device available to determine any deficiencies within the participative systems is what is referred to as a "union vulnerability audit". This type of audit, sometimes referred to as a "personnel audit", is an independent evaluation by a labor relations specialist who checks each and every facet of the employer's various employee programs. Many attorneys and consultants have devised their own techniques for conducting such an audit. (For example, the author has designed a copyrighted Union Vulnerability Audit which is coordinated to the ten Master

Keys discussed in this book and entitled "A Union Vulnerability Audit for the Union Free Employer".)

Although the union vulnerability audit can be conducted internally by the employee relations manager or some other member of the management team, the results are achieved more objectively through the services of a qualified expert who can independently evaluate the systems and design a specific plan of action to overcome any deficiencies.

Employers that spend thousands of dollars per year for such auditing services as accounting, inventory or purchasing should be equally committed to spend the necessary money and effort to audit their vulnerability to a union attack and to establish or bolster programs which preclude a union drive.

This chapter has been devoted to the participation necessary to build teamwork and a family relationship among all of the employees within a **Union Free** *establishment. The* **Union Free** *philosophy is that employees who belong to the overall team and enjoy and appreciate being members of that team will not desire to become an adversary party by joining with an opposing force such as a union.*

Union Free employers should implement as many of these communications and employee programs into its facility as possible. Moreover, the **Union Free** employer should not be satisfied with the examples discussed here but should fashion its own programs in keeping with the nature of its business, its services, its customers and its location.

Such sound and properly administered participative programs and systems should create the desired atmosphere of teamwork instead of an atmosphere of hostility associated with a unionized employer.

The participative management concept is the heartbeat of a **Union Free** environment.

Chapter 6

The Right Of Review

The Master Keys discussed in Chapters 6 and 7 may well be captioned "Taking It Away From The Union."

Unions typically exploit two weaknesses of many non-union employers. They proclaim that the employees do not have meaningful grievance procedures and equally propagandize that the respective employees do not have job security.

This chapter addresses the necessity for a meaningful grievance procedure and Chapter 7 discusses the urgency of honoring such job security essentials as seniority rights of employees. When a **Union Free** employer has successful programs regarding grievances and job security, the union's propaganda falls on deaf ears.

The sixth Master Key to maintaining **Union Free** *status is a sound and responsive procedure through which employees may protest any adverse action taken against them.*

The many communications and employee programs discussed in Chapter 5 should serve as substantial "safety valves" to ventilate employee gripes and complaints.

Assuming the various programs previously discussed were adopted by an employer, an employee could voice his complaint in several ways.

He could bring his complaint to the attention of his supervisor in the daily or weekly "staff meeting." He could anonymously place his concern in the "complaint box." The employee might choose to "unload" his discontent upon the employee relations manager during a "rap" session.

He might prefer to bring the matter to the attention of the employee relations manager during an "on-the-floor" interview or discuss the matter during his periodic interview if it is not of an urgency nature. The attitude survey may be the vehicle utilized to voice his concern or he might wish to "phone" his complaint, via the "hot line".

Although these programs should address a vast majority of employee complaints, more is needed to defeat the union's traditional claim that the employer does not have a responsive grievance procedure.

The **Union Free** employer should therefore implement two different traditionally-designed grievance procedures and systems.

He should first adopt an informal system known as the "open door" policy and he should thereafter implement a formal grievance procedure with the traditional safeguards of appealing to higher officials until the matter is either resolved or exhausted.

THE "OPEN DOOR" POLICY

The "open door" policy is a most beneficial approach to grievance handling. The **Union Free** "open door" policy assures the employee of the right to take his problem or complaint directly to anyone in management, including the chief administrator and the employee relations manager, after informing his supervisor that he so desires to meet with a higher management member.

The most important element in the "open door" concept is that the doors of management must truly be open. If there is too much red tape injected into the system, the employee who might otherwise use it will be "turned off" by the mechanics involved and possibly use other "methods" to voice his grievance, such as taking them to a union organizer.

All levels of management should therefore be committed to the "open door" policy and make themselves freely available.

Sufficient time and attention should be given the dissatisfied employee so that he will not gain the negative impression that his discussion is an exercise in futility.

The "open door" policy should establish timetables for the manager's response to the employee. Many **Union Free** employers use a 24-hour period in which to investigate and get back to the employee either with an answer to his inquiry or to inform him that additional time is needed to better investigate and fully evaluate the matter. It is most important to honor the 24-hour response period, and resort to extensions as infrequently as possible. However, if additional time is absolutely needed, it is mandatory that a new time period be specifically established and communicated to the employee in question.

The most perplexing problem with an "open door" system is its "off the record" rejection by front-line supervisors.

Lower level supervisors often frown upon the "open door" system because it allows employees to "go over their heads" to higher management.

Supervisors who are substantially deficient in good supervisory techniques, and supervisors who are "playing games" with their employees should fear the "open door" because the system will surely find them out. Supervisors who have built the proverbial "empire" in their section see the "open door" policy as a constant threat to their creation.

The fact of the matter is that the "open door" policy really does allow an employee to go "over the head" of the supervisor. That is its very purpose. Without a very liberal system through which employees can circumvent unresponsive or arbitrary supervisory practices, the employee is blocked from vertical ventilation of his problem and must use horizontal channels to relieve his frustration. Horizontal communication to voice complaints has many pitfalls; there are no "pluses".

When the employee is impeded from vertical communications his inclination will be first to communicate his frustrtion among his fellow employees. When they are likewise subjected to the same system, the problem is compounded because of their identification and empathy with the complaining employee.

The employee will surely communicate his grievance to his family. He may also discuss it with his friends outside the facility. He may seek advice or counsel from his minister, priest or rabbi concerning his grievance.

He may feel the nature of his grievance is of such interest to the community that he will write a letter to the local newspaper or bring the matter to the attention of the publisher, which results in a newspaper article on the subject--particularly if it pertains to some controversial item such as health care, safety, environmental controls or some other sensitive topic.

The more people he talks to, the more the odds are increased that he will hear suggestions that a union may be the only answer to his problem. "Union" "Union" "Union" may become a ringing sensation in his ears.

He may be even more direct. Instead of discussing the matter with various individuals, his first horizontal contact may be the union.

Will a **Union Free** employer force an employee into such an alternative route? Will a **Union Free** employer keep a policy of "backing supervisors" to the extent that an employee cannot get around arbitrary and capricious foremen? **NEVER!**

A **Union Free** employer will not only have an "open door" policy, the door will be open. A **Union Free** employer will inform its supervisory and management team that an interference or encroachment upon an employee's right to use the "open door" review system will subject the supervisor — not the employees — to strong disciplinary action, perhaps discharge.

A **Union Free** employer will explain the full responsibilities and obligations to the supervisor.

The **Union Free** employer will educate the supervisor so that he will not fear the "open door" system, but welcome it. The "open door" relief valve will enlighten middle and higher management on areas of weakness on the part of supervisors so that special training can be directed towards shoring up those deficiencies.

When the supervisor understands that the system is in reality a valuable aid to his growth as a supervisor and an enhancement to his promotional opportunities, the fear on his part should be eliminated.

The **Union Free** employer should also inform the front-line supervisors that they have a joint role in the "open door" system. That joint responsibility is not only to appreciate the system and encourage its usefulness but additionally to be accessible so that the employee may have an opportunity to discuss the grievance or complaint with the supervisor first. (The better "open door" policy does not require that the employee *must* discuss his problem first with the supervisor before going to higher management.)

The **Union Free** supervisor should understand that the "open door" concept is a "piece of cake" compared to the grievance system typically found in many collective bargaining contracts, in which a union shop steward might second guess a supervisor's every act.

The **Union Free** employer can ill afford to back a supervisor whether he is "right" or "wrong". Supporting a "wrong" supervisor in disregard of an employee's fair treatment is a sure means—a guaranteed means—of bringing a union into the organization.

The open door policy is a method by which to uncover supervisors who have acted improperly and affords the management team an opportunity to correct those "wrongs", either by schooling the supervisor on the "right" methods or eliminating him from the team if he will not respond to the "right" methods.

The "open door" policy should be publicized and reinforced on a continuous basis, from the initial orientation process to the retirement banquet.

FORMAL GRIEVANCE PROCEDURE

It is debatable whether a formal grievance procedure is always necessary, as a practicable matter, when the "open door" concept is actively used and employees freely communicate their unrest and frustrations through such programs as the "rap session" or the periodic interview. Employees most likely would not go to the additional effort of initiating formal grievances and the mechanics they entail when they may easily accomplish the same objective through the "open door".

Yet, a formal grievance procedure provides the employee an additional avenue to process his appeal of an adverse action to several individuals of the higher echelon. It affords the employee some special attention and documentation that might not be present in the "open door" or other systems.

Above all, it takes away the argument of the union that such grievance procedures are not available for the employee.

Most formalized grievance procedures, both in **Union Free** and unionized operations, consist of several steps of review by various individuals in the management chain of command. Unlike the traditional steps in union contracts where specific time limitations are set for the employee to process his grievance in lieu of waiving his rights thereafter, **Union Free** formal grievance procedures should not be so regimented.

The difference between the union conceptualized grievance procedure and the mechanics of the **Union Free** grievance procedure is shown by the final stage of each.

Arbitration is the unionized final phase, with all the accompanying costs and emotional strain. On the other hand, the **Union Free** final step involves a review and consideration by some internal committee, normally from the management team, or the top administrator of the facility. Because of the differences in the final step and the fact that the **Union Free** employer is not subjected to the costs and exposure of possible reinstatement and backpay found in the unionized grievance procedures, rigid timetables for the **Union Free** employees should not be applied.

The mechanics of the **Union Free** grievance procedure involve five essential elements.

The first element is that it should be explained in written form in the employee handbook as well as publicized through other communications media. Its publication should not be overdone, however, because the "open door" system should be the primary outlet for employee grievances; the formalized method should be secondary. Nonetheless, the formalized system must be fully communicated and occasionally reiterated to the rank and file employees.

The second element involves the supervisor's role or the first step of the formalized procedure. In most **Union Free** systems, the supervisor receives a formal complaint from the employee either by written document or verbally communicated, which constitutes the first step of the procedure. The supervisor has an obligation of attempting to resolve the formal grievance at that stage without thwarting the employee from appealing to the second step if the employee is not completely satisfied.

Most **Union Free** trained supervisors who are fair but firm in their management style and who have administered policies in an equitable and consistent manner are able to resolve the grievance at this point.

The third element involves the right of the employee to appeal the grievance from the supervisor to someone in middle management such as a department head, or in a smaller operation, perhaps to the employee relations director. Again, all efforts should be made to adjust the grievance in keeping with consistent practices and good management. Particularly should the employee relations director use sophisticated personnel techniques to resolve the grievance. He should do no less whether he is directly involved in the sequence of appeals or is involved from the sidelines in earlier or later steps.

The fourth element involves the use of a grievance committee or a top official for final review. The infusion of a grievance committee lends a certain degree of "fair play" to the procedure, the theory being that a collective review might be more judicial than an individual one.

One note of caution should be mentioned at this point concerning grievance committees. Many **Union Free** institutions and businesses become enthralled with the inclusion of employee participation into the grievance process. When employees are given the power and authority to adjust grievances on behalf of other employees and management recognizes a group of employees as a collective body in adjusting grievances, the arrangement might be considered as a "company dominated union" in violation of Section 8(a)(2) of the National Labor Relations Act. Therefore, particular care should be taken in allowing employees to participate in the formalized grievance system.

Other **Union Free** employers select a mixture of employees and management to comprise the grievance committee which might also border on violating the NLRA—depending on the authority given to the employees.

Most **Union Free** employers do not include employees in the grievance committee. It certainly is not necessary and normally creates more problems than it eliminates.

Many **Union Free** employers that have sound open door policies and other communication programs through which employees can redress their grievances do not bother with grievance committees. They simply use the top official at the facility for the final review.

The final element in the formalized grievance procedure is the requisite objectivity needed at each phase of the procedure. If the employee has been "wronged", it should be made right. If the policy is wrong, it should be changed.

Fair play is the underlying theme of both the "open door" and the more formal approach to the grievance solving process.

Chapter 7

Employee Rights

During a union campaign, the union is most likely to inject the theme that it offers employees "job security". The phrase has a potent implication.

Employees are impressed that some outside force can assure them security in their jobs, especially if such employees are insecure in their relationship with the employer.

However, a union's reference to "job security" is a misnomer and is very misleading.

When a union forces an employer into a strike and the employer replaces the employees, resulting in the loss of their jobs, the union has destroyed the employees' job security instead of enhancing it.

When a union's unrealistic demands have driven the costs of the operation up to a point that the employer is uncompetitive and it is forced to close its doors, resulting in the employees' job loss, the union has cost the employees their job security instead of improving it.

If an employer produces a seasonal product which requires layoffs for a certain period of time each year, a union has no power or means to secure a job for the employees during the "down time". If a recession "hits" which requires a substantial layoff of employees a union has no "magic pill" by which to get the employees back to work.

The union has no power or influence to assure the employee of any real job security. The employer is the only entity that can provide jobs for the employee.

The use of the phrase "job security" by the union is misrepresentative. The Union utilizes the phrase in reference to traditional employee rights typically safeguarded in a union contract.

When a **Union Free** employer safeguards traditional employee rights, it counteracts the union promise of "job security".

Thus, the seventh ingredient in a **Union Free** *environment is the requirement that traditional employee rights are protected through fair and equitable policies.*

SENIORITY

Union Free employers should first assure protection of the seniority rights of their employees.

PROMOTIONS AND TRANSFERS

The fact that a **Union Free** employer honors the length of continuous service of employees should not decrease its qualitative or quantitative standards.

Seniority must have limitations or otherwise a "30 year" janitor would be president of the organization.

A **Union Free** employer must protect its reputation of a good service or product by requiring requisite skills and abilities (and possibly other qualifications) before seniority may apply in the promotion or transfer to a higher paying or more prestigious position.

A job bidding system is utilized by many **Union Free** employers in promotions and transfers to assure that seniority rights of its employees are protected.

The job bidding system involves the posting of a job opening notice on the employer's bulletin board or in some other way publicizing it to the employees. An employee interested in the job has the opportunity of placing his name in consideration for the new position. The employee who has the most seniority and has the requisite qualifications to fulfill the position is given first chance to perform the job.

There are other requirements in a bid system, such as that an employee can only move from one position to another after a certain duration or that an employee will be returned to his old position if he cannot perform the new task.

The bid system is a most important tool in recognizing seniority rights of employees and precludes employees' arguments that they were not given an opportunity for some certain opening.

Bid systems should be sparingly used in the promotion of employees into the managerial ranks for reasons set forth in Chapter 2.

LAYOFFS AND RECALLS

Seniority should likewise be given consideration when employees are laid off and when there is a recall.

A requirement that a senior employee also have the requisite qualifications in order to "bump" a less senior employee into the layoff pool protects the integrity and quality of job performance.

The recall system should also require the skills and abilities to do the job.

Some **Union Free** organizations have tied other qualifications into the layoff and recall procedure, particularly when there are no appreciable differences in employees' years of service, in an effort to keep the most productive employees and assure the highest productivity.

Such factors as past performance records, attendance records and disciplinary records are given weight in the layoff/recall procedure. Seniority is used, however, as a tie-breaker when employees have comparable records.

OVERTIME

Although some employers attempt to distribute overtime work among employees on an equal basis, a better policy is to give the more senior employees first refusal. Seniority rights are protected and many older employees do not want the overtime in the first place. A failure to offer them the opportunity, however, only leaves disgruntled employees to later complain that their seniority rights were not honored.

When there is an insufficient number of volunteer employees to accomplish the overtime tasks, then the less senior employees should be called upon with reverse seniority applied.

MISCELLANEOUS SENIORITY RIGHTS

More senior employees should be given the first opportunity to schedule their vacations, assuming that the facility is not completely shut down during the vacation period.

Seniority should be recognized in shift preferences. Seniority should also be recognized in additional fringe benefits such as more vacation time for longer service.

Longevity awards discussed in Chapter 5 are an important attribute in recognizing length of continuous service of the employee.

STANDARDS OF PERFORMANCE

Another anxiety on the part of employees concerns standards of performance. Whether the employees' performance is subject to an objective measurement such as "parts per hour" or is of an immeasurable quantity, fair play must exist.

Employee rights include reasonable guidelines in establishing standards of performance and objective guidelines by which to evaluate an individual's performance.

Industrial engineers and other personnel who establish production measurements should therefore be tuned in to the **Union Free** principle of fair play.

Union Free management should closely monitor employee reaction to substantial overtime or pressurized production commitments and find methods to relieve the employee of anxiety.

HEALTH AND SAFETY

Another employee right is that of a safe and healthy work place. The Occupational Health and Safety Act (OSHA) has placed certain mandatory requirements (some of which are unreasonable) on most employers to insure the safety of employees on the job.

The **Union Free** employer must view its obligation from more than a legal standpoint, however. It should have a genuine and sincere interest in the safety of its employees and should manifest that interest through an educational and monitoring approach.

AFFIRMATIVE ACTION

Most union contracts protect employees from discrimination because of race, sex, religion, color or national origin as well as age.

The union contracts merely reiterate what is legally required of an employer, with or without the union.

The **Union Free** employer should equally publish and communicate its affirmative action policies to its employees. Moreover, it should monitor its programs to assure equal rights to all employees.

Union Free employers provide the traditional employee rights to their employees, that are normally outlined in a union contract. They do so for more than the mere reason to "take the argument away from the union"; they do so because of *fair play.*

Chapter 8

Elimination of Employee Irritants

"Elephants don't kill you, the gnats do" is a cliche analogous to the labor relations rule that "little things will do you in, not necessarily the big ones."

Sources of continuous irritation are the "gnats" that frequently bring about unions, either directly or indirectly.

The eighth key to maintaining a **Union Free** *environment is the elimination of sources of constant irritation that grate upon your employees' sensitivities over a long period of time.*

Employees may not feel the urge to go directly to a union because of long standing "pet peeves" but may well respond to an approach by a union organizer in the hope of obtaining some type of relief.

Many unions use a collective list of employees' "pet peeves" as a means of stirring up union support and identifying common problems that the employer has left unattended. The union's "sales pitch" is that it will make the employer respond to such problems.

Union Free employers must give special attention to the "gnats" in their organization and accentuate communications programs such as the "rap session" illustrated in Chapter 5 to discover the "little" problems as well as the "big" problems.

Many employees will not approach their supervisors or other members of management about smaller things that constantly bother them for fear that management will think they are "nit-picking", but the aggravation will continue nonetheless.

Simply because employee irritants appear to be diminutive in nature is little reason to ignore the fact that they exist. Whether small or large in the eyes of the management team, continuous irritations are leading factors in union victories.

Their elimination is essential to maintaining **Union Free** status.

WORKING CONDITIONS

Employees appreciate their jobs more and perform more efficiently when they work in a clean, pleasant and attractive atmosphere.

Union Free employers understand that satisfied employees make productive employees and productive employees are the most important resource they have.

A satisfied work force can partially be achieved through an attractive work climate. Special attention should be given to the following areas to eliminate as many employee irritants as possible.

REST ROOMS

The **Union Free** facility should have modern rest rooms and adequate janitorial services to keep them clean, bright and sanitary.

Untidy and dirty rest rooms become even more untidy because employees do not take any pride in assuring their cleanliness. On the other hand, clean and sanitary rest rooms create a pride in the employees so that they, in turn, will pay more attention to their own personal habits.

Adequate toilet tissue and paper towels, or some other drying equipment must be available. Likewise, women's rest rooms should contain a well stocked sanitary napkin dispenser.

The rest rooms should be properly ventilated, deodorized and well lighted. They should contain hot water and adequate soap.

Rest rooms are very important to employees. Sensitivities surrounding personal habits are very profound.

Union Free employers also understand that employee rest rooms are sometimes used in union organization attempts. Pro-union employees are encouraged by unions to use the rest rooms as their headquarters in "signing up" additional employees into the union, especially when the rest rooms are not commonly shared by management and rank and file personnel. (Possibly more union authorization cards are signed in employee rest rooms than all other places combined, including the union halls.)

The **Union Free** employer should require its management team to use the same rest room facilities as other employees. This practice not only thwarts union efforts due to the presence of supervisory and management personnel, but equally removes the management trappings attached to separate facilities, as discussed in Chapter 2.

EATING AREAS AND BREAK ROOMS

Many **Union Free** employers do not have the personnel or facilities to provide hot meals for employees and must rely upon vending machines in their lunch rooms and break areas.

Nothing irritates the author more than to place a coin in a vending machine and receive nothing in return—not even the coin!

Vending machines can cause nightmares for the **Union Free** employer if they do not function properly.

Employees are normally tired and hungry when meal time approaches during their shift. Both mentally and physically, they are looking forward to a refreshing respite. Consequently, if the vending equipment malfunctions, the agitation and disappointment is severe on the part of the employee.

He may well be disposed to take his resentment out against his employer for failure to have the equipment in working order. He assumes that his employer does not care for his physical and emotional well-being.

Many vending companies are very attentive to their customers and provide an attendant in larger facilities to monitor the machines and keep them well stocked. The **Union Free** employer must make sure that it has the best vending services available and must communicate its efforts to the employees. It must back up that commitment and accept nothing but the best from its vending supplier.

The **Union Free** employer must implement a method of reimbursing employees for coins lost in vending machines; it should guarantee that the machines are properly stocked with a variety of foods and beverages and that the hot foods are "hot" and the cold items are "cold".

It should assure the employee of a clean, sanitary and pleasant atmosphere in which to rest and eat. The lunch/break area should be well lighted and comfortably ventilated. Even though the working areas may not be air conditioned or heated due to the nature of the work or to cost factors, the area in which employees have a few minutes a day to relax and eat should be.

PARKING FACILITIES

Another recurring irritant with many employees is the lack of sufficient parking space at their employer's premises.

Union Free employers have the obligation to prevent such aggravation by (1) providing adequate spaces for all employees who desire to park their vehicles at the facility; (2) keeping the parking areas well lighted for the safety and security of the employee and his property; (3) removing all obstacles which might interfere with the employee's safe passage; (4) paving the parking surface to eliminate "mud" holes and other rough surfaces; and (5) marking and "lining" the parking area so that the traffic flow will be easy and efficient.

WATER FOUNTAINS

Thirst is another human condition which, when left unsatisfied, can create intense annoyance.

The **Union Free** employer should make sure there are plenty of water fountains in the working areas. He should assure that the water is of pure quality and cool.

He should make sure that the fountains are in good working order and that the surrounding areas are sanitary and clean. A trash container should be strategically placed near the fountains for the disposal of chewing gum, candy wrappers, and cigarette packages.

FIRST-AID ROOM

When an employee is injured or becomes ill on the job, he is naturally in an irritable mood. A lack of first-aid care in addition to being dangerously irresponsible, compounds that irritation and creates additional bitterness on the part of the employee.

Union Free employers consequently must provide basic first-aid services for the protection and comfort of their employees.

If possible, the employer should furnish a first-aid room, or at least designate an area for such a purpose. The area should be clean and contain a cot or bed.

The designated area should contain a lavatory and hot water. If possible, the **Union Free** employer should stock the first-aid room with more sophisticated medical supplies for critical emergencies such as burns and heart attacks and have non-ambulatory supports such as stretchers or wheel chairs. Many larger facilities employ a full-time nurse or para-medic to administer first-aid and maintain the first-aid facilities. If possible, such a person should be employed. If it is not feasible to employ such a person, then the **Union Free** employer should insure that someone at the facility is trained to administer first-aid.

TOOLS AND EQUIPMENT

Employees who desire to do a good job are sometimes handicapped by lack of adequate tools and equipment.

This situation can lead to intense dissatisfaction on the employees' part, especially if they are on some paid incentive system and lack of equipment cuts into their pay.

Union Free employers must make all efforts to supply employees with the necessary tools by which to do their jobs and maintain a credible position by fully explaining any temporary inadequacies.

Not only should the **Union Free** employer provide sufficient tools and equipment, it should assure that they remain in sound repair and good working order.

HOUSEKEEPING

Employees become aggravated when housekeeping methods infringe upon their comfort and safety.

Closing of rest rooms for several hours so they can be cleaned at the janitor's convenience can have a most irritating effect.

Wet and greasy floors over which employees must tread can be equally alarming.

Trash, toxic chemicals, defective parts and so forth, which are unnecessarily located close to an employee's work station may well create an unnerving effect.

Aisles and corridors that are blocked by misplaced goods or equipment are additional "downers" for employees.

The **Union Free** employer should have adequate janitorial services and housekeeping rules to eliminate such disturbing conditions. It must do everything reasonably possible to make physical working areas an attractive part of the work climate.

MISCELLANEOUS IRRITANTS

Some employees like the temperature hot and some like it cool;

some like country music, some like "rock and roll" and some like none; some like close supervision and others desire no supervisor at all.

The differences in the "personal" desires of individuals can create additional friction in the work place. To overcome this friction, the **Union Free** employer should be attentive to individual preferences and do everything reasonably possible to accommodate them or work out compromise solutions.

The fact that the employee is comfortable will improve his attitude and his efficiency as well.

It might be that the employee desires to bring a pillow to raise him higher in his chair for better comfort and easier work. Why not? (Better yet, the employer should furnish it.)

It might be that an employee desires an electric fan or air conditioner duct turned in another direction to relieve his sinus condition. Why not?

In each case, the **Union Free** employer should accommodate the employee as long as such accommodation does not adversely affect other employees or interfere with the work process.

Scheduling is another of the prevailing sources of aggravations.

When an employee has planned a week-end trip with his family and not informed until Friday afternoon that he will be required to work overtime on Saturday, the employer has just created a monstrous and justifiable "peeve". A failure to notify employees of shift changes and other scheduling modifications at the earliest possible time makes a lasting negative impression in the employee's mind.

The lack of clarity in a policy or instruction, resulting in an employee's failure to understand it, provokes additional concern.

The list could go on and on. The primary point to remember is not the list of "pet peeves" and sources of constant irritation discussed, but rather, that each **Union Free** employer should continually ask itself, "What are the constant and specific aggravations in our own facility?"

The failure to ask that question and to take corrective action if called for may well determine whether a union is going to be in a position to send a swarm of "gnats" flying back at an employer having already convinced its employees that it can do something about these constant irritations.

Chapter 9

Elimination of Undesirable Personnel

As death begins at birth, so employee termination begins at hire.

Termination may come about during the probationary period, after several years of employment, or upon retirement—but termination occurs at some point.

The ninth step of **Union Free** *status is the prompt elimination of employees and supervisors who do not meet the standards of the* **Union Free** *employer.*

There are many potential dangers in terminating employees both from legal and practical considerations. The **Union Free** employer must understand both.

The **Union Free** employer should be knowledgeable of the Civil Rights Act of 1964, Title VII, which precludes discharge (as well as other actions taken against employees) on the basis of race, sex, religion, color and national origin. It should be aware of the Age Discrimination in Employment Act (ADEA) which presently precludes discharge because of age in the protected age group between 40 and 65, and will extend protection to employees up to 70 years of age as of January 1, 1979.

The **Union Free** employer should fully appreciate the impact of the retaliation sections of the Fair Labor Standards Act, Occupational Health and Safety Act, National Labor Relations Act, Equal Pay Act and other labor relations laws that make it illegal to discharge an employee as a result of his filing a complaint with the agency enforcing the respective law.

The **Union Free** employer may have other similar obligations respecting discharges if it is a federal contractor or receives grants or other monies from federal or state agencies. In addition, the employer may fall within the jurisdiction of some state or municipal regulation requiring non-discriminatory action with regard to its discharge policy.

Above all, the **Union Free** employer should understand the laws regarding discharge under the National Labor Relations Act.

Section 7 of the National Labor Relations Act, as amended, states that employees have the federally protected right to self-organize, to join or assist unions, and to bargain collectively through a union. Employees also have the right *to engage in other concerted activities for the purpose of collective bargaining or other mutual aid or protection.* Finally, employees have the right to refrain from all such activities.

Although most laymen are under the impression that the National Labor Relations Act and the Board which administers it are only involved when there is some union activity, the law also extends protection to employees who engage in "concerted activities" without the presence of union influence or association.

While this book is not intended as a legal treatise, but rather as a guidebook in maintaining **Union Free** status, the understanding and appreciation of the interrelationship between labor relations law and **Union Free** philosophy is essential to achieve the non-union objective.

The legal protection of "concerted activities" of employees simply means that an employer, within the jurisdiction of the National Labor Relations Act, cannot legally discharge or otherwise discriminate against two or more employees who band together in some manner to protest wages, hours, or some other terms or conditions of employment, even though there is no union involved.

The law also extends protection to an individual employee who makes similar protests on behalf of a group of employees.

Certainly, under specific conditions, the employer can permanently replace employees who, as a group, refuse to work due to such protests—but discharge, as distinguished from permanent replacement, is legally proscribed.

When an employer is faced with such a condition he should contact his labor relations attorney immediately for proper counseling. Of course, the **Union Free** employer should also check with its counsel concerning Title VII, the Age Discrimination in Employment Act, or all other labor relations laws that preclude discriminatory or retaliatory discharges when it is unsure of its legal posture.

More frequent than legal battles over discharges arising when employees file charges with the National Labor Relations Board alleging that their discharge resulted from participation in protected "concerted activities" are those which arise from charges alleging that a discharge was for union activities.

Certainly, no employer—not even the employer operating under the **Union Free** philosophy—is immune from having unfair labor practice charges filed against it, particularly in response to a discharge. Inasmuch as the **Union Free** employer may be the victim of unfair labor practice charges, it should understand the basic elements of proof which must be established to sustain a charge of illegal discharge which may be filed against it.

The first element which must be proven to sustain a charge alleging discharge for union activities is that the employee was in fact involved in union activities.

Secondly, it must be proven that the employer had knowledge of the employee's union activities. Obviously, an employer can't be said to have discharged an employee for union activities unless it is shown that the employer *knew* that the employee had union involvement.

The third element which must be proven is that the employer, in discharging the employee, treated him differently from other employees in similar circumstances. This element is generally referred to in the law as "disparate treatment".

The fourth element is termed "animus" and relates to the motive of the employer in the discharge and to the attitude of the employer toward unions generally.

If it can be shown that "but for" the employee's union activity he would not have been discharged, the requisite anti-union motive can be satisfied. Likewise, if it can be shown that the employer harbors hostility against unions or maintains a posture of keeping unions out of its facility, the motive element is satisfied based upon the theory that had the employer been favorably disposed toward unions, it obviously would not have discharged an employee favorable to a union.

Theoretically, all four elements must be proven against the employer before it will be found in violation of the National Labor Relations Act. In practice, the National Labor Relations Board and many of its Administrative Law Judges use a liberal dose of inferences instead of more traditionally accepted evidentiary facts to sustain a case against an employer.

In this regard, then, the **Union Free** employer should be especially mindful of the role "timing" can play in sustaining a case of illegal discharge against it. The National Labor Relations Board looks very suspiciously at an employer that discharges an employee during a union campaign.

When discharges occur at such times, most employers seek to justify their action by showing that the employee was fired for good cause, for example, insubordination, or poor work performance or attendance.

In such cases it is not uncommon to hear the employer comment that he should have gotten rid of the employee months or years earlier because of the offensive conduct, but that he simply never got around to it.

Had the employer discharged the employee earlier because of his unsatisfactory conduct, there probably would have been no basis for the unfair labor practice charge and the employer would not need to face the emotional strain of attempting to justify its position. Moreover, the employer would not have to face the fact that his very tolerance and condonation of the employee's previous failings may well be used to prove the case against him.

Thus, it is imperative that the **Union Free** employer recognize the importance of eliminating unsatisfactory employees from its work force at the earliest possible stage.

The process of eliminating managerial and problem employees begins with the probationary period. If during such period or at its conclusion there is genuine doubt that the employee can measure up to the employer's standards and especially if the employee, despite careful screening, has exhibited behavioral traits described earlier in Chapter 3, the **Union Free** employer must have the "guts" to terminate such an employee.

In this regard, it is the responsibility of the entire management team and most particularly of the specific supervisor and employee relations manager, to recognize their obligation to preserve the high quality of the employee complement.

That is not to say that each and every employee should not be given full opportunity and the necessary training by which to accomplish his assigned job. It does mean that "problem" employees frequently surface during the probationary period and if it appears that the employee will not make the "grade", it is much better to face up to that fact then and terminate the employee at the earliest time possible. (Contrary to some lay impressions, a probationary employee has the same protection under the National Labor Relations Act and other labor relations laws, as does the more senior employee).

As mentioned, the **Union Free** employer should understand the practical consequences of discharge in addition to the legal ramifications.

Obviously, an employee may be discharged for any reason which is not proscribed by the various federal, state or local employment discrimination laws. However, the **Union Free** employer recognizes that in the employer/employee relationship, discharge constitutes "capital punishment". Thus, the **Union Free** employer is sensitive to the employee unrest and insecurity which discharge can generate.

The most beneficial practical consequence of discharging an employee at an early date, as opposed to an employee with several years seniority, is that insecurity is not created in the remaining employees.

Most employees who are responsible and dedicated do not desire that a "good off" or "insubordinate" employee continue on the payroll. As part of their identification with participative management, they empathize with the employer's decision to terminate such an employee at an early date and welcome the decision. That is, they do if the employee who is discharged is relatively new.

However, if the employer discharges an employee who has been "on board" for several years, even with some long term deficiencies in performance, some employees will identify with the discharged employee rather than with the employer.

This is not to suggest that long term "problem" employees should not be terminated. They indeed should be terminated if they have not become reliable and productive employees. The point is simply that the longer an unproductive or marginal employee (or some other undesirable employee) is allowed to remain with the employer, the less the remaining employees will be likely to accept the discharge as a rational and fair one.

Sometimes the discharge of an employee can generate a feeling among fellow employees to the effect that the discharged employee is in some way a "martyr". This is especially true if the discharged employee is very popular and his discharge is suspect in the eyes of a large percentage of the remaining rank and file members.

The "martyr" phenomenon often is initiated by a union to gain support for its cause. A union may in fact purposely coach a pro-union employee into getting himself discharged, and, thereafter, propagandize that the employee was discharged unfairly. The union is then in a position to further spread propaganda that without the union's so-called protection the remaining employees' jobs are equally in jeopardy.

In summary, the **Union Free** employer when discharging an employee, must protect itself against the possibility of job insecurity and/or "martyr" backlash. This can be done by following certain self-imposed principles.

The first principle is that it must have its rules of conduct and related policies properly published and distributed to all employees as outlined in Chapter 4.

The second principle is that the rules and policies must be consistently enforced.

The third principle is that the facts and circumstances relating to the reasons for discharge must be fully documented.

The fourth principle is that the employer should discharge deficient employees at the earliest possible stage if it appears inevitable that such will be the later course of action.

The fifth principle is that the employer must communicate its reasons for terminating a certain employee to those remaining employees who may be critical of the decision. This is a most important move because "rumor mills" can quickly mislead employees and can turn the matter into the "martyr" situation.

The sixth principle is that the employer should establish a discharge checklist and educate each and every management member to follow it religiously. The following is a sample discharge checklist which might be considered:

SIXTEEN STEPS TO FOLLOW BEFORE DISCHARGING AN EMPLOYEE

1. Suspend the employee and initiate a thorough investigation in order to get all the facts (unless there are absolutely no facts in dispute and the conduct calls for summary dismissal).

2. Get *all* the facts including any remarks the employee in question might care to make.

3. Determine whether there is a rule or policy which calls for dismissal based upon the facts involved.

4. Determine whether the employee was aware of the rule or policy in question.

5. Determine whether there have been any exceptions to the rule or policy.

6. If there have been exceptions, determine if the factual situation at hand fits any of the exceptions.

7. If this is the first discharge case under a particular rule, double check the original purpose and intent of the rule and confirm that it is still a timely and proper one.

8. If the employee in question is a minority or some other class protected employee, insure there are no disparate applications of the rule relating to the protected characteristics.

9. If the discharge has been brought about because the last step in the progressive disciplinary procedure has been reached, recheck to make sure that all past steps or procedures have been properly followed.

10. Make sure the employee is not engaged in any type of protected concerted activity.

11. Determine whether the discharge will make the employee a "martyr" and, if so, set up communication plans to overcome the effect of such "martyrdom".

12. Make sure that the employee's file has proper documentation and witnesses to support the discharge case.

13. At the time of actual discharge, make sure there is another managerial employee present.

14. At the time of discharge, be short and brief without references to sympathy or "passing the buck".

15. If at all possible, reference the specific rule of conduct which has been violated, but otherwise draft the description of the reason for discharge in very general terms.

16. Make sure that the procedures utilized in conducting the discharge and exit of the employee are the same as those utilized in previous discharges.

To be sure, this chapter has thus far dealt with the discharging of rank and file employees. However, the **Union Free** employer must also recognize its obligation to promptly eliminate from the management team deficient supervisors or managers who either cannot or will not reform their substandard practice.

Normally, the discharge of a supervisor does not create the anxiety and insecurity in the rank and file which might occur in the case of the termination of a fellow employee. In fact, when the supervisor possesses such negative characteristics as those described in Chapter 2, the employees will most likely welcome the change. Nevertheless, the discharge of a supervisor may create the same job insecurity and "martyr" effects which the discharge of long-term employees can generate. Thus, the **Union Free** employer should be mindful of these possibilities and seek to counteract them if they should arise among the rank and file or among fellow supervisors.

The author realizes that his recommendations to eliminate undesirable and unsatisfactory employees and supervisors might find disfavor with the behavioral scientist who might feel that all employees and supervisors can be "saved". The author is not suggesting that the **Union Free** employer refrain from attempting to help the deficient employee or supervisor conform to its standards. The **Union Free** employer does, in fact, have that responsibility and should afford the deficient employee and supervisor every possible educational tool and instructional device available.

But when the deficient employee or supervisor does not change after such training and attention, the **Union Free** philosophy dictates that such employee or supervisor be terminated.

Chapter 10

Equitable Wages and Fringe Benefits

There is good reason why a discussion of wages and fringe benefits appears in the last chapter of this book.

One might suggest that this subject matter should be discussed in the first chapter on the premise that wages and fringe benefits are surely the primary reasons why employees resort to unions. However, such a premise is not valid.

Most union campaigns are not brought about because of wages and fringe benefits. In fact, very few are.

That is not to say that money is not a major issue in most union campaigns. It is. It simply means that wages and fringe benefits are not the driving force behind the initial union push.

Whether the wage and fringe benefit issue will be a determinant one in a union drive will depend to a large degree on the fairness of these wages and benefits and their equitable administration.

When an employer can show its employees that it is paying at least an average rate of pay and fringe benefits compared with like businesses or institutions and when the employees have no genuine complaint about the internal administration of the wage and fringe benefit program, the employee is in a *good* position to counteract the union's propaganda about getting the employees substantially more money and benefits.

When an employee is paying higher wages and has a better fringe benefit program than competitive unionized employers, it is in a *great* position to overcome the union's propaganda. The employer can simply argue—"If the union is going to do all that for you, why hasn't it done it for employees it already represents?"

Therefore, the tenth (and final) ingredient to maintaining a Union Free *posture is that the* Union Free *employer must have a competitive wage and fringe benefit program that is equitably administered.*

WAGES

"Equal pay for equal work" is a maxim which if followed will serve the **Union Free** employer well from a legal perspective. It is a must to staying non-union.

Unions capitalize on employers that have a reputation of wage inequities.

Employees will understand and accept, as equitable, wage differentials based upon four conditions, and four conditions only:

(1) **LONGEVITY.** Most employees understand a system in which employees with longer service receive more wages as a result of their seniority, even though the younger employees are doing the same work as the more senior employees and all are equally proficient in their jobs. Equity is indirectly built into the system because the less senior employees will eventually receive the higher wage and will have something to look forward to in the future.

(2) **EQUITABLE CLASSIFICATIONS.** Employees readily accept the fact that a skilled electrician should make more money than a janitor at the facility. As long as the various classifications or labor grades are properly structured, most employees will have few problems in accepting the policy of higher wages for harder or more skilled work or more responsibility.

(3) **MEASURED INCENTIVE.** Employees do not find fault with incentive systems that provide more money for more work produced. An acceptable incentive system, however, must have measurable controls to determine the qualitative or quantitative results of an employee's efforts.

(4) **SHIFT DIFFERENTIALS OR SPECIAL CIRCUMSTANCES.** When an employee must work at a less desirable time or in a less desirable location, other employees generally agree that such employee should gain some additional money for his inconvenience, even though the job itself might be the same. Shift differentials are an example of this and many **Union Free** employers give such additional pay.

MERIT SYSTEMS

Many non-union organizations stress the value of a merit system so that employees may be justly rewarded for their special efforts.

However, few union contracts contain a merit system of pay. There is a good reason why union representatives dislike traditional merit increases. It is not because of their disapproval of the principle of more pay for better performance. Rather, it is a distaste for the administrative defects typically found in the system, such as susceptibility to inequities based on the biases or favoritism of some supervisors and managers.

The **Union Free** employer should be equally dubious about merit increases.

Merit systems which rely heavily upon subjective evaluation by management personnel are filled with potential trouble.

Assume, for example, that a particular supervisor has ten employees under his direction and that he has been handed an evaluation sheet to complete in order for the employees to get merit increases ranging from $.15 to $.30. The employees perform the same jobs and have been with the employer for approximately the same number of years. The supervisor is to "grade" the employees on such subjective criteria as "cooperation", "disposition", "appearance", "attitude", and "initiative" and then recommend raises based upon his evaluations.

As a result of his recommendations, two employees are given $.15 raises, seven employees are given $.20 raises, two employees are given $.25 raises and the remaining employee is given a $.30 raise.

How many of the employees will be disgruntled over their increases? Most, if not everyone except the employee who received $.30.

First, unless there is a markedly (and admittedly) poorer performance on the part of the employees receiving the lower pay increases of $.15 and $.20, the lower paid employees will proclaim that they did equally good work as the ones receiving the higher pay. The two employees who received $.25 will each feel subconsciously that perhaps they should not have received more than the $.15 and $.20 employees, but they will almost routinely outwardly express a "cry" to their supervisor that they should have received the $.30 increase. Perhaps the employee who received the $.30 increase will be happy with his raise but he may well compound the confusion by stating, out of empathy with the rest, that all employees should have received the $.30 increase.

This might be an extreme example. However, it does illustrate that an employer that bases increases on subjective factors frequently winds up making its employees "sad" instead of "glad".

The argument is normally made by the "pro-merit school" that the merit system can be redeemed through the utilization of objective standards instead of subjective ones. This is probably true, and such a system may well find employee acceptance. This result will occur because if truly objective criteria are utilized, the "merit system" then becomes a "measured incentive" system, the third category of acceptable basis for wage differentials discussed above.

However, it must be noted that it is almost impossible to objectively measure and exhaust many non-repetitive jobs. For example, what objective measuring tools can be used by which to evaluate the performance of a nursing assistant who may perform a variety of tasks from one day to another? How does one measure the quality or quantity of work of a repair mechanic who may be called upon to do numerous tasks, none of which are repeated in the course of a week or possibly months?

The fact is that without some solid data derived from accurate measurement of quantity or quality results, the merit system will inevitably be applied subjectively.

Union Free employers pay close attention to the underlying reasons why unions back away from subjective merit systems. Most **Union Free** employers simply do not use any merit related system that cannot be administered totally through the use of objective standards.

CLASSIFICATIONS AND LABOR GRADES

One of the most important considerations in wage administration is that wages must be equitably administered internally, for example, from one classification to another as well as within a specific classification.

An employer could pay an average wage rate of twenty dollars per hour, a scale many times the rate of pay of its union and non-union competitors, and still be unionized because of wages.

Assume that a particular employer had two classifications in which comparable work was being performed but in one classification employees received $25 per hour, and in the other, employees received "only" $15 per hour. Further, assume there were fifty employees who received the lower scale and only five who received the higher rate.

Such an employer could rest assured that the fifty employees making the lower pay would be responsive to a union's "sales pitch" that the union would get them parity with their higher paid counterparts.

Union Free employers must therefore ascertain that their classifications and labor grades are structured in keeping with modern methods and are based upon sound and equitable principles.

Many **Union Free** employers attempt to classify jobs and pay differentials into as few categories as possible and allow the job bidding system to position the more senior employees, with the requisite qualifications, into the more favored jobs within the category. This is normally a sound philosophy where the nature of the work is similar throughout the facility and there are no substantial differences in the skills, responsibilities and efforts required in the various jobs.

WAGE STRUCTURES

In addition to the need to properly and equitably classify employees into wage categories and labor grades, there is the question of longevity and what increases, if any, should be based upon seniority.

Many **Union Free** employers structure wage programs as follows:

(1) An entry rate of pay is established for each classification or job category.
(2) The new employee receives a pay increase at the end of his probationary period.
(3) The employee receives a pay raise at the end of his first year.
(4) He receives a raise at the end of his second year.
(5) Possibly at the end of his third or fourth year he receives another raise.

These raises are frequently referred to as "longevity" or "seniority" raises. They do not include annual increases or "across the board" increases which normally are given to all employees irrespective of their years of service with the employer.

Most longevity raises "top out", both with unionized employers and non-union employers, after a few years in order to maintain an acceptable differential among all employees doing the same job.

Most employees find longevity raises equitable because each has the same opportunity of receiving them based upon seniority.

DURATION AND AMOUNT

The **Union Free** employer should show its employees that it has a policy of continually monitoring and reviewing wages, and further, that its employees will continue to receive wages and fringe benefit increases.

The employees should be secure in the knowledge that they have not reached the "end" of their pay progression, but will receive additional wages in the future.

Union Free employers should constantly survey comparable union and non-union businesses or institutions in their geographical area to determine what are competitive wages and salaries for positions and job categories within their organization. The **Union Free** employer strives to be in the "ballpark" with its wage and fringe benefit programs, and preferably to exceed those of unionized employers.

Many **Union Free** employers grant increases at the same time each year. This system provides a measure of security for the employees and gives them something to look forward to each year. It precludes the fear on the part of the employees of being "dead ended".

Periodic increases also provide the **Union Free** employer with a legal defense if there is a union campaign going on when it gives the raise. (Employers who do not have such a system and grant wage increases during a union campaign may be subject to a National Labor Relations Board complaint that they gave the increase to thwart the union drive.)

The amount of the increase should vary from period to period but not get out of balance at any one time. Employees who are accustomed to receiving twenty to thirty cent increases annually and then receive a fifty cent raise in a one year period may infer that they will continue to get annual increases of fifty cents in future years.

FRINGE BENEFITS

The **Union Free** employer should be as attentive to its employee fringe benefit program as it is to its wage policies.

An important labor relations theory that should be adopted by **Union Free** employers is that employees appreciate being informed of potential fringe benefits and some possible time tables for their implementation even if it is not feasible for them to be implemented immediately.

Another important concept is that employees respond to an employer's plight of needing to start off "light" in a few fringe program areas if there is the prospect that they will be extended and expanded at a later date. Thus, in the area of fringe benefits "form" can be as important as "substance".

There are many fringe benefits that **Union Free** employers should have in their package. They include the following:

HEALTH INSURANCE

Although an employer may not be financially able to pay for the most sophisticated medical plan available, **Union Free** employers should provide some basic coverage for their employees. Few, if any, union contracts do not have some type of health insurance.

HOLIDAYS

Union Free employers should provide time off with pay on all traditional holidays and should make an effort to observe holidays which may be recognized locally. In the case of holidays it is especially beneficial to stay ahead of unionized competitors and neighbors when possible.

VACATIONS

Union Free employers should not only have a competitive vacation plan, but should make sure the plan is clear and administratively functional.

The plan should recognize seniority in some way by providing more vacation time for more senior employees with reference to some specific seniority dates.

LEAVES OF ABSENCE

Although employees may not feel that leaves of absence are fringe benefits, the **Union Free** employer should educate its employees that they are additional fringe benefits because such leaves are a handicap to the employer and not all employers allow them unless legally required.

Standards should be established through which leaves will be granted and these standards should not be compromised.

JURY DUTY PAY

The cost of jury duty pay is relatively inexpensive and is required by law in several states.

The pay is generally the difference between what the employee receives from the Court and what he would have made had he been able to work.

FUNERAL PAY

Most **Union Free** employers pay employees for a limited number of days they are required to be off as a result of a death in their immediate family.

Most union contracts provide for such benefits and the **Union Free** employer should do no less. Funeral pay may well be an area where an employer can start off with a "light" program and build upon it by announcing improvements from time to time.

SICK DAYS

The **Union Free** employer should have a sick leave policy and allow employees off so many days over a certain period of time for medical reasons. Again, sick leave may be an area in which a "light" program can be utilized to bring the benefit into existence and subsequent improvements can be the basis for announcements of improved benefits.

SHIFT DIFFERENTIALS

Although the employee might view the shift differential as only pay, it should be communicated as an additional fringe benefit for it surely is for those who receive it. The **Union Free** employer should pay such differentials when employee inconvenience is involved.

LIFE INSURANCE

Term life insurance policies normally accompany group health insurance. If policies do not include life insurance, it is relatively inexpensive to acquire smaller amounts of life coverage. Some form of life insurance should be implemented as an additional fringe benefit of the **Union Free** employer.

There are numerous other benefits which could be added to the foregoing list, such as profit sharing or retirement plans. Depending on the nature of the work of the employer, some may be feasible and some may not.

Nevertheless, the **Union Free** employer should attempt to implement as many and varied fringe benefits as possible—and surely more than its unionized counterparts. In particular, it should develop and implement some fringe benefits that are peculiar to its own operation.

The employees should be told the additional costs, in raw cents per hour, of their fringe benefits and this information should frequently be communicated to them through such devices as pay envelope stuffers.

And finally, fringe benefits should be implemented and improved at varied times, not necessarily at the same time as periodic wage increases are given. Such staggered implementation can be utilized to boost employee morale at critical points when it lowers, for example, between wage increases or at times when the work load is especially heavy.

Wage and fringe benefits can be said to be "neutral" influences in most union campaigns when the **Union Free** employer has competitive wages and fringe benefits that are equitably administered. Frankly, the employer does not generally gain overwhelming support as a result of its positive position because in the eyes of its employees, it is doing exactly what it is supposed to do. The real benefit derives from the fact that a union cannot convincingly attack the employer on the issue of wages and fringe benefit programs.

However, when the non-union employer is marginal or substandard in its wage and fringe benefit plans, then its fringe benefits will surely have a substantial "negative" impact on the employer as a union will invariably exploit this weakness and be able to gain support as a result.

Summary

What you have read is not based upon theory. What you have read is not based upon behavioral science experimentation.

What you have read is based upon a decade of pragmatic observations on the "battle fields" of where counter-union campaigns have been fought.

The **Union Free** employers that had adopted and practiced the "Ten Master Keys to Maintaining Non-Union Status" won their private wars.

Many **Union Free** employers repelled the initial union seige because their employees believed that they had been treated fairly and, therefore, refused to sign union authorization cards or give any other aid and comfort to the enemy.

Other **Union Free** employers experienced the "full battle" and were victorious in their National Labor Relations Board elections.

The **Union Free** employers that were victorious in defeating the union attack had paid the "price" in terms of money, time and effort in their commitments to maintaining a **Union Free** atmosphere.

The victorious **Union Free** employers had screened, selected and trained the highest caliber supervisory and management personnel. Many of these managers and supervisors received "battle field" commissions because of their outstanding performances in turning back the union forces. Others won an assortment of personal commendations.

The victorious **Union Free** employers had equally selected a legion of positive, dedicated, responsible and reliable employees who measured up to the call of duty.

The "fox holes" of the victorious **Union Free** employers reflected fair and equitable policies, rules and regulations which had been published and distributed to employees.

The victorious **Union Free** employers had an assortment of communications and employee programs that resulted in an outstanding "esprit de corps" among the **Union Free** forces.

The **Union Free** fortresses were not exposed to the unions' "battle cry" that the employers had failed to afford their employees the rights of "seniority", "job security" and "grievance procedures" because the employers had previously made such honored rights secure.

The **Union Free** "trenches" revealed few lingering employee irritations and, therefore, the unions were unsuccessful in their efforts to attract many sympathizers to their cause.

The victorious **Union Free** employers' major conquests were made when they were able to show their employees that they had paid better wages and provided more benefits than could be found in the unions' own collective bargaining contracts with unionized employers.

Although victorious in defeating the unions' attacks, many **Union Free** employers had their casualty lists.

The "body count" included personnel directors who had compromised their screening procedure and who didn't take the time to do the necessary background reference check on a host of employees who were later exploited by the unions' forces.

Among the casualties were a cadre of supervisors who had built their own personal "empires" and left dishonest and inconsistent habits as their legacy.

A few leaders also died in the wars. One manager who seemingly "drove a chariot" over his subjects fell at the "Battle of Credibility". An administrator met her demise at the "Battle of Unfilled Promises."

There were some **Union Free** owners and stockholders who, although not mortally wounded, were severely injured because their management teams had not been responsive to their employees' needs or complaints and the ensuing "Battle of Resentment" was a most intense one.

But out of all the battles and wars, the **Union Free** philosophy stood "tall"; the integrity of the **Union Free** concepts were preserved. The **Union Free** flag waved proudly in the end.

The non-union employer is invited to join the ranks of the **Union Free**. To do so, however, it must be committed to adopt and live by the "Ten Master Keys". The motive which will sustain that effort will not be merely a desire to remain non-union, but rather the sure knowledge that the implementation of **Union Free** principles will result in a more satisfying, harmonious , and profitable work experience for all concerned.